The Vedic God Mitra

A Concise Study

The Vedic God Mitra

A Concise Study

Marta Vannucci

D.K. Printworld (P) Ltd.
Publishers of Indian Traditions

Cataloging in Publication Data — DK
[Courtesy: D.K. Agencies (P) Ltd. <docinfo@dkagencies.com>]

Vannucci, M. (Marta), 1921-
The Vedic god Mitra : a concise study / Marta Vannucci.
p. cm.
Includes bibliographical references (p.) and index.
ISBN 13: 9788124605868

1. Mitra (Hindu deity) 2. Hindu gods in literature. 3. Vedic literature — History and criticism. I. Title.

DDC 294.5211 22

First published in India, 2011
ISBN 13: 978-81-246-0586-8 (HB) ISBN 10: 81-246-0586-6

Published and printed by:
D.K. Printworld (P) Ltd.
Regd. office : *'Srikunj,'* F-52, Bali Nagar
Ramesh Nagar Metro Station
New Delhi – 110 015
Phones : (011) 2545 3975; 2546 6019; *Fax* : (011) 2546 5926
E-mail: indology@dkprintworld.com
Web: www.dkprintworld.com

Dedication

To the memory of my Mother

and all Mothers

Acknowledgement

PARTICULARLY helpful for this study was the repeatedly quoted book and other papers by Bhargava (2001) to which I often had recourse. I also wish to acknowledge with gratitude the support and encouragement given by three friends who are directly responsible for the writing of this book. Whatever merit there may be in it is due to them, I only had to write down my thoughts. I am grateful to Carlo Manzini, my *mitra* (friend), for his literary knowledge, his care and guidance; to Jenny Haslett for her remarks and bibliographic help and to Filippo Gambassi who first raised a key question about God Mitra, for his sensibility and for his always-clear critical appraisal and encouragement. The excellent "Glossario Sanscrito" published by Asram Vidya, Rome, has been liberally used for writing the present Index. Finally, last but not least I wish to offer sincere thanks to Monica Zavattaro and Maria Gloria Roselli of the Anthropologic and Ethnological Section of the Museum of Natural History of the University of Florence, for their professional support and technical help.

To Mr Susheel Mittal I am ever indebted for his unfailing support for the publication of this book, for his perseverance to have it carefully edited, for his ever present care and above all for his constant patience with this author.

Contents

List of Illustrations

fig 1. Imprint of a seal of the Hittite king Suppiluliuma 1st of Hatti (capital city Hattusha), middle fourteenth century BCE. See Guidotti and Daddi, 2002.

fig 2. Line drawing of the imprint of a seal of Suppiluliuma of Hatti. Reading from up downwards, highest is the solar disc which is above all Creation; under the solar disc there is a saddle-shaped seat with a flowing wing on either side. Under the seat the drawing of a belt buckle or necklace clasp (?). I would interpret the two wings as representing Mitra (Law and Justice) and Mazda (Light, Warmth). The symbol as a whole represents Ahura-Mazda or *Hvarshed (=kwarshed, Xvar-Xsahita* (Might, Splendour), the word *ahura* in Skt. corresponds to the Greek *daimon* a *Being* gifted with exceptional power and competence that he may use for good or bad.

fig. 3. Gold square "necklace button" with Ahura-Mazda shown on the "saddle" here covered by the side panel of the king's robe, from "The Hermitage", St. Petersburg; *see* Dandamayev, 1996, pre-Zarathustra period. Lining by Anna Maria Bedini.

fig. 4. Signet ring with winged lion, *see* Dandamayev, 1996, from "The Hermitage", St. Petersburg. The item is perhaps contemporary with that of *fig*. 3, probably pre-Zarathustra period. Lining by Anna Maria Bedini.

fig. 5. Achaemenid king Darius 1st (558?-486? BCE) of Persia receiving a line of prisoners with a foot on a prostrated captive and the right hand held in a gesture of command. Ahura-Mazda surveys the scene from above (*see* Dandamayev, 1996).

fig. 6. Rock relief of the Investiture of Ardashir 1st at Naqsh-i-Rustam (year CE 224 or 227 — *see* Litvinsky et al., 1996; Chegini et al., 1996). The relief shows the *magus* at the extreme left waving the *barsom* and wafting the good spirit or aroma over Ardashir who holds the symbolic ring with the right hand on the opposite side and together with Ahura-Mazda.

fig. 7. Imprint from a cylinder seal showing a hunting scene with the name of Darius 1st. Ahura-Mazda with widespread wings hovers over the scene. According to authors the cuneiform script at left is probably in Aramaic language. Specially interesting details: the harnessing of the two horses, the special structure of the chariot, the shoes on the wheel and the date-palm trees.

fig. 8. *Dexiosis*. The hand-clasp between Mitra and the Sun-god. *From* Ossanna 1998, front cover.

fig. 9. Tauroctony, the killing of the bull: Tauroctony, sculpture found on the altar of a mithraeum excavated under the Basilica of St. Clement in Rome: courtesy of J. Haslett.

fig. 10. Photo of the *barsom*, contemporary specimen made of 35 metal filaments, one of them thicker, tied together with a vegetable fine string. The bundle rests horizontally over two tall metal supports placed one at each end of the bundle of "twigs". Courtesy of the Section of Anthropology and Ethnology of the Museum of Natural History of the University of Florence, Italy.

1

Introduction

My colleague Filippo Gambassi and I recently discussed various aspects of the transfer of culture among different people of Central Asia (Vannucci, 1998, 1999, 2007, forthcoming). Gambassi raised the specific question of the semi-secret establishment in Rome and elsewhere in the Empire and in the Graeco-Roman world of temples devoted to an imported god called Mithra. The so-called Mithraeum (pl. = Mithraea) flourished in Rome from the middle of the last century BCE onwards and were centres for the meetings of a select religious community well into CE times, only to disappear as quietly as they had come, during the decadence and the riotous disorders that followed the fall of the Western Roman Empire in CE 476 or somewhat later, until the descent of the Longobards in peninsular Italy in CE 568.

To better understand the rise, activities and closure of the Mithraea in Rome, we pushed our study back in time as far as historical and mythological knowledge could take us. The Vedas and the *Avesta* on one side and the Mediterranean, Greek, Roman and Central Asian history on the other were the starting points of our work.

The present study is centred on the figure of Vedic God Mitra, a reserved, quiet and almost self-effacing personality who was nevertheless ever present for the proper fulfilment of important civil and religious acts and duties. Though somewhat mysterious, Mitra was highly respected, revered and invoked for his truthfulness, reliability, knowledge and power. The most salient attribute of Mitra is his constant association with Varuṇa, the only unbound, unfettered son of Aditi, mother of Infinity and The Infinite herself. In fact, Varuṇa is more often mentioned in association with Mitra than alone. Mitra is mentioned 175 times in the *Ṛgveda* alone and about 20 times under the dual Mitra/Varuṇau. Mitra is described as wonderful, glorious, mighty, brilliant, endowed with golden splendour.

Varuṇa, the free and great son of Aditi is her first "born" (= originated, created, produced, begotten hence called "sons") of the original seven Ādityas. Varuṇa and Mitra were followed by Bhaga, Aryamān, Dakṣa, Aṁśa, Sūrya each with its own attributes and field of competence or *timai* in Greek, as in Hesiod. Bhaga is the god who distributes wealth according to merits and demerits of each one of us. Aryamān is the prototype of the noble Man, the Lord of men and *pitṛ*s (ancestors). Dakṣa is the learned and able craftsman, the creative inventor. Aṁśa is *a* portion or *a specific* or *an allotted* portion of a whole. Sūrya is the Sun-God giver of light, warmth and life, over time Sūrya becomes the close associate of Mitra. Thus Mitra became partly identified with Savitṛ, the essence, concept or principle of the Sun. In *Ṛgveda* VIII. 41 and I, LXXXIX Bhaga/God is called Bhagavān, the form used down to present.

Indian and Iranian mythologies as well as the oral tradition of the Indo-Aryan and Indo-Iranian people are particularly interesting from the cultural viewpoint. They are best studied and understood under their anthropological, ecological and philosophical aspects, as much as from their religious and social significance. The oral and later the written tradition of the ancient-most Indo-European clans, who all called themselves *Arya*, has remained unbroken in India down to present since their early days and mythology (Vannucci, 2007). With time and following displacements, the corpus of ancient, rich and detailed traditional knowledge gradually incorporated new myths, new empirical and new scientific and historical knowledge. They were codified and evolved as philosophies beyond religious beliefs in India as Vedism and Hinduism at large and in ancient Iran and Persia as Mazdeism and Zoroastrianism. There are probably nowhere else cultures that have as long and unbroken tradition beginning since the most ancient nebulous past, all the way down to present. The oral tradition, mythology and folklore, habits and customs have survived, specially in India over millennia of unbroken evolution, development, additions, deletions, corrections and interpolations as nowhere else.

These studies offer the opportunity to go back in time to a stage when the thoughts and reasoning of Man were still anchored in Nature about which Man felt to be himself a constituent part. I interpret the word Man, written with a capital M, as a being conscious of having a conscience.[1] The evolution of the mind and of consciousness, the invention of technicalities, the development of science and philosophy in the ancient Greek sense of the word, evolved with time everywhere in the world; however the Indo-Aryans and Indo-Iranians developed differently between them and from most other people. A characteristic trait of the Indian culture is that no knowledge, factual or speculative, was ever discarded. Teachings of sages, scientists, philosophers or just revered elders were remembered and consigned to the collective memory of the people "because it could be true or not, who knows?" (*R̥V* X 129, 6/7, tr. Griffith) meaning that they should be preserved for future valuation if any.

6. Who verily knows it and who can here declare it, whence it was born and whence comes this creation?

   The gods are later than this world's production.

   who knows then whence it came into being?

7. He, the first origin of this creation, whether he formed it all or did not form it,

   What eye controls this world in highest heaven,

he verily knows it, or perhaps he knows not.
— (Ṛṣi Prajāpatī Parameṣṭhin), tr. Griffith

Every bit of knowledge was kept to be eventually eroded away, changed, modified or retained by cultural selection or newly-acquired knowledge. The cultural evolution of the original Indo-Aryan and Indo-Iranian people who over the millennia mixed with other cultures and people, can be followed through the folklore and through the immense corpus of written texts available in Sanskrit, Avestic and derived languages, everywhere in the habitable world of those past eras, as well as in modern languages. The habit of putting in written form sacred, epic and profane texts was developed very late but the incredible feat of memorising all texts of historical, philosophical or religious interest had become one of the perfunctory duties of the learned brāhmaṇas and of the *magi*. In early ancient times among the Indo-Aryans in India and the Indo-Iranians in Central Asia there was no conceptual difference between sacred and profane, everything in this world is sacred anyhow, for the simple reason that it exists. Knowledge was and still is stored in the collective memory of the people and is known as "oral tradition"; it includes also mythology, fables and technical know-how. Even the ancient Indo-Iranian insistence to condemn the *daeva* of the Indo-Aryans was an indirect factor for the preservation of the oral tradition of all the Arya people. The memory of the old myths and folklore was preserved throughout the Zoroastrian/ Mazdeian and Sassanid periods (third to middle seventh centuries CE). It is still present as late as Firdausi's *Shahnameh*, even if in a somewhat changed garb.

This book is a synthetic look at the origin and evolution of the personality of *Mitra*, a most significant representative of the early stages of the story and culture of the Indo-Aryan and Indo-Iranian clans whose presence and competence are defined since the early period of their presence as nomadic tribes who came from the Eurasian steppes north of the Black and Caspian Seas and roamed far and wide over Central Asia. Their culture was preserved as oral tradition, semantics, artefacts, sciences, poetry, music, iconography, engineering and technicalities as well as daily know-how, family life, social habits, customs, and legislation.

2

The Name and Personality of Vedic God Mitra

THE name Mitra occurs in 175 hymns of the *R̥V*, and at almost 20 places as the compound Mitra/Varuṇau in the *R̥V* alone, in addition to an entire hymn dedicated exclusively to Mitra. Sāyaṇa spells Mitra=*mitrā*. In the *Avesta* as it has come down to us, the name is written *Mythra* or *Mithra* in middle Persian, also called Pahlavī. It is present in contemporary languages as the god of Mithraism which was an imported locally heterodox religion that flourished since the last century BCE far and wide in the Empire and Mithraism was practised in all the Graeco-Roman world well into the fifth/sixth centuries CE.

In Italian the word *mitra* comes from Latin *mitra* or *mitria* that in turn comes from Greek *mitra* (*apud* Devoto, 1968). The Latin words *mitera* or *mitria* also come from Greek *mitra* (=Persian *mithra*) that was the name of the formal headdress of the emperors of ancient Persia. The word *mitra* in Latin and Greek was originally the name of the sacred headband worn by high priests of various religions when performing particularly sacred rites. The English word *meter* (metre) comes from Latin *metrum* and Greek *metron* where the root syllable *mee* is cognate of the Greek word *meetis* (=wisdom and measure, involving also psychological overtones). The onomatopoetic syllables *ma* and *mah* suggest Care, Greatness and Wonder.[2]

The same meanings of the syllable *me* is present also in Germanic and some Indian languages. The use of sacred headbands, ribbons or strings worn by the officiating priests, pilgrims and faithful devotees of several religions survives down to present also in many contemporary cultures. They may be worn during the performance of sacred rites and rituals by the officiating priests, participants or postulants. A common example could be the popular expression "tying the knot", meaning to get married in the ritual of Hindu marriage where this simple gesture is performed once at a predetermined point of the rite.

The words *metrum, mensura,* in Latin have a similar implication by insisting on the importance and sacredness of the act of performing and judging material or physical values such as measuring fields and grounds, assessing all types of measurements or validating the "wisdom" or opportunity of applying defined acts, restrictions or promotions to something or anything.

The original meaning of the Sanskrit word *mitra* is "friend", a beloved companion, with the full implication of truthfulness, faithfulness, reliability, honesty, friendliness and love. One has unconditional belief and faith in a true friend. A friend is an entity, a "being" that deserves to be called *MITR* or *MITRA* because of his precision and punctiliousness in performing duties and keeping promises, for offering help unconditionally down to the ultimate details, provided those acts fall within the sacred "jurisdiction" or *timai* of the god and within the code of laws of *ṛta.* The term "jurisdiction" is used here with the same meaning as *timai* in Greek, meaning the "field of action, the duties and competence of the god" (*see* Vannucci, forthcoming). It is god Mitra who validates treaties and contracts. Such a friend inspires devotion, fidelity, love and obedience. God Mitra is a friend and a true friend is Mitra, this is still the meaning of the word in present-day good Hindi.[3]

In Pahlavī the name *mitra* becomes *mithra*=companion, a word that in Latin and in Greek originally meant "one with whom we eat together," or: "with whom we share the same food," a person whom one trusts completely, a comrade and advocate, a reliable confidant of men who can bear witness and preside over the writing and keeping of alliances and contracts. In the *Avesta*, Mitra is one of the Great Judges who sit on the *Cinvat* bridge where the souls of the deceased are judged before being allowed — or not — to enter into the Netherworld. A historical example of the power of Mitra is the role that his Name and his virtual presence played in the drafting of the peace treaty between the Indo-Aryan Hittites and the Egyptian pharaoh Ramses II after the Battle of Qadesh, 1275 BCE (Vannucci, 2007).

Problems of semantics are met with at every step when trying to enter into the mind of the men of millennia ago. All translations use indifferently words such as "god" and "king" though they do not carry exactly the same meaning throughout the Vedas or in the contemporary wording. In ancient times the words *king* and *god* were used as synonyms because they initially did not have a social or political connotation. They expressed man's awe, respect and admiration for the personality talked about, usually the leader. Gradually a notable personality was addressed as king to mark that he was the most powerful member of the clan, tribe or group on the move that needs a successful leader. The king may later become a god through an euhemeristic process. Indra is a typical example of an euhemeristic deity, a skilled leader of the Indo-Aryan tribes whose image survived age after age. The bull is a ready-made symbol of power and strength to be found throughout the Indo-European and other cultures. Mitra is occasionally praised as the *bull*. Much later Mithraism associates the young bull to god Mithra and the animal is sacrificed to honour the god. The best approach to the study of Vedic God Mitra is to recognise that the basic sense of the name has not changed throughout the centuries. The Sanskrit word *mitra* meaning a special friend or, using present-day words, Mitra is a "bosom friend" well alive even after the Industrial Revolution.

Mitra, like the other Ādityas, existed since the beginning of time and earlier than other gods. To illustrate what Mitra represents even at present the best words could be, though none gives the full meaning of the name Mitra: *closeness, sympathy, sharing the same emotions even if painful.* The name Mitra may perhaps at present be mentally realised in terms of the physical/chemical/biological sense of the words *affinity, resonance, amity, similarity, alliance, mental and emotional correspondence.*

Mitra gradually, from being a Light and Sky God, grew to be seen also as Good Provider of the means that enable man to perform correctly the appropriate rituals and rites (*Ṛ̥V* V.III, 59, 9):

> Mitra to Gods, to living man,
> To him who strews the sacred grass,
> Gives food fulfilling sacred Law.

The foremost auspicious grass is the *kuśa* grass some blades of which are strewn on the ground consecrated for the performance of ordained rituals and sacrifices. The word "food" is to be understood here both as spiritual and holy food as well as food for the body, namely the food that became available in plenty after the development of agriculture. After hunting, domesticating animals and stock breeding, the most important step forward towards growth and acculturation was the practice of methodical agriculture.

This happened many centuries prior to the transfer of Demeter from Central Asia to Attica in Greece (Vannucci, 1998) thanks to the support given, if not by Heracles himself, certainly by the tribe of the very strong Heraclides. But that is another story given by detail and much exuberance in the *Dionysiacs* by Nonnos (fourth-fifth century CE), a very long poem to be read with one or two pinches of salt and chronological corrections.

3

The Origin and Evolution

ADITI is the originator of the Ādityas (= those who come from Aditi) who share with her a common life principle. Originally there were seven Ādityas, they represent the primordial basic Vedic principles or gods, both natural and man-made later. With cultural development and growing knowledge over the centuries the number of the Ādityas grew to 12. These principles are personifications of ideas or basic concepts, they are personalised as characters to facilitate the thinking and reasoning of the human mind. Mitra was always related to Justice and to "The Law and Rules" that govern all humans, whether nomads or settled.

Hillebrandt (1980/81) defines Aditi (neutral) as the "eternal light with its abode in the sky, Ādityas being the sons of this light . . . where the concept of light emerges from the concept of freedom from bondage . . . and is opposite not only to darkness and of restraint from want as well." To this partial interpretation of what Aditi stands for I would add that Mitra, her "son", is the Āditya who is also a light/solar god who puts Life in motion, because there is no life without movements and vibrations.

Thus the primordial attribute, or *timai,* of Mitra is to recognise, uphold and protect the world of Varuṇa, the great *asura*, the unfettered "son" of Aditi. Aditi, the "mother of infinity", is herself (itself) the personification of the concept of Infinite; she is unbound, unfettered, unrestrained, unlimited because she is also the guardian of the entire cosmos. Aditi is limitless *beyond understanding*. However, Varuṇa, Mitra and the other gods are eternal, but not infinite. Varuṇa is not bound by fetters, but he has them in his hands and uses his whip to punish the wicked men whom Mitra has judged and condemned. In both the Vedas and the *Avesta* the existence of the gods is said to be limited to the present *kalpa* after which their time will be exhausted and they will disappear, they are therefore eternal but not infinite.

Varuṇa in the *ṚV* and elsewhere in the ancient texts is more often quoted in association with Mitra than alone. Varuṇa is the first of the original seven Ādityas originated by Aditi. He is usually quoted as the "unfettered" (fetters = *pāśas*) or "unbound" "son" of Aditi, meaning that Varuṇa alone among the Ādityas was created and remained forever unbound, though he holds the fetters with which he ties up sinful persons. Varuṇa, the great *asura* (Ṛgvedic *asura* = Avestic *ahura*) is eternal, unlimited, boundless but not infinite. Eternal means covering a long time/ space *continuum* but something eternal may come to an end. Differently, the concept of infinite is that of something endless at both ends of the time/space *continuum*. A physicist specialised in dimensional analysis would define the term "eternal" as something that has no *temporal* limitations, while the term "infinite" is defined as something that has *mass, dimension, time*. Strictly speaking, the word *infinite* describes something that has no spatial limits, and is therefore limitless. The term *eternal* refers to something that has no temporal limits but may or will eventually come to an end. These terms apply to both material and immaterial realities and are used throughout this essay in this sense. The two terms "eternal" and "infinite" are in no way synonymous (*Ṛgveda* I. 139, 2):

> As there ye, Mitra, Varuṇa, above the true have taken to yourselves the untrue
> With your mind, with wisdom's mental energy,
> So in the seats wherein ye dwell have we beheld the Golden One,

Not with our thoughts or spirit, but with these
our eyes, yes, with the eyes that Soma gives.
— Ṛṣi Parucchepa, tr. Griffith

On the strength also of other commentators Griffith clarifies: " . . . the poet says: 'With our bodily eyes we have seen the Sun, but enlightened by the *soma* juice we have recognised it as being only an image of you.'" In *Ṛgveda* I.25.20 Varuṇa is given also the epithet of *medhira* (=wise, *apud* Bhargava 2001).

The name Varuṇa may be read as "the one who encompasses everything" or "that contains the universe." As defined by the name, Varuṇa is limited by its own nature, while Aditi is boundless in space and time, she is limitless and she is the personification of an idea, a concept, an entity called Infinite. Varuṇa is the great and powerful lord who encloses the lands and waters of this world in his spiritual domain. With time Varuṇa became known as the god who regulates the water cycles of the skies and of Mother Earth. Varuṇa is the Lord who reigns supreme over the laws of nature and over the laws made by man. Mitra is faithfulness personified and the guardian and voucher of the Laws of Varuṇa of both the physical and virtual worlds. Quoting from *Ṛgveda* VIII. IV. 52.3a Vālakhilya hymn:

यस्मै विष्णुस्त्रीणि पदा उप मित्रस्य धर्मभिः
yasmai viṣṇustrīṇi padā upa mitrasya dharmabhiḥ

He to whom Viṣṇu came striding his three wide steps, as Mitra's statutes ordered it. — Ṛṣi Srustigu, tr. Griffith, p. 468

Mitra's jurisdiction and field of action covers, oversees and is responsible for the maintenance of order and law in Varuṇa's domain. The terms "eternal" and "infinite" refer to material, immaterial or virtual realities of this world and of the entire universe. Varuṇa and Mitra, as well as the other Ādityas exist since the beginning of time and are "earlier" than other gods, as mentioned in the Vedas.

Aditi the universal mother has the power to release others from bonds and represents — or IS the universe or cosmos. Her name is the ancient-most word that we know of at present that was used in ancient Sanskrit to designate the *Originator* or *Creator, Infinity* itself, she is everlasting. Aditi is the mental representation of E*ssence* or *Existence* itself, hence the term "mother" who is the only *human being* on Earth capable of producing a new *being* similar to itself. Yet, her "sons" were begotten, not made. In translation Aditi is best rendered as having no ends ever. The word eternal is expressed by finite numbers, while the word infinite is represented by irrational numbers. The easiest way to realise mentally the word infinite is the Fibonacci number, whose symbol is the Greek letter *phi*. I am grateful to Prof. Armando Brissoni who took great pain to teach me the mathematical difference between the words "eternal" and "infinite" that are expressed by different equations.

In the modern literature the terms *eternal* and *infinite* are often applied indifferently and inadequately to Aditi, Varuṇa, Mitra and others. Like other gods, Mitra and Varuṇa are *eternal* but only Aditi is *infinite*. In both the Vedas and the *Avesta* the existence of the gods ends with the present *kalpa,* they are therefore *eternal* but not *infinite.* In Vedic terms the *universe* or *cosmos* exists in space and time wherever and forever and its symbols and numbers cannot be expressed as positive integers because *man has no sure knowledge* of their origin or beginning and no *sure* idea of their end.

Throughout his long career as an archetype Mitra is bound by fetters that represent the limitations imposed on man by his consciousness. Mitra is the personification of rectitude, integrity, truthfulness, moral excellence, probity, uprightness. Mitra represents the strict obedience to the Cosmic Law; however, in real life there are no simple or easy ways to solve ethical or moral problems or situations. Varuṇa is eternal, unbound though not limitless. Varuṇa's existence will last as long as man will have and will listen to his conscience. Internal, moral or psychological conflicts that occur in man's mind or when man feels that he cannot be both this and/or that, instinctively redirect man towards the two most ancient archetypes, the bound and the unbound, Mitra and Varuṇa. It is then that each individual must bear the responsibility to decide on the course of his own actions. In Jung's words (2006: 288), "conflicts of duties and responsibilities can only be solved by each one of us individually and again at every time when the conflict arises . . . whenever we must take a moral decision we should not succumb to either of the two opposites: good and bad." There is no absolute good or bad and Mitra's help is invoked when difficult decisions must be taken. This is why Mitra is man's greatest friend.

With time Varuṇa becomes concerned with waters, the most essential element of Nature together with the Sun and the Moon. Waters and Sun, Varuṇa and Mitra (later also Savitṛ) are the essential powers whose energy creates and maintains Life on Earth.

4

The Cultural and Religious Aspects

THE Ādityas originated by Aditi are forms, abstract principles that take shape and grow in one's mind. They create and mould what I would call in Latin: the *forma mentis*, the sum total of virtual realities that derive as an inescapable deduction from the existence of Aditi and Varuṇa her first "son". Mitra's attributes are his intrinsic order and logics as well as physical and virtual measurements and measures that he applies as he watches each person and mankind as a whole. Like other Ādityas except Varuṇa, Mitra is not unbound or eternal, he is limited by fetters, he is the guardian of the Law, of the natural and the universal laws of the finite world of Varuṇa. Mitra rules over the human people, whether nomads or settled, he is the god who sustains and enforces obedience to the Cosmic Law. As such he is the most reliable friend of human beings, he should be emulated, believed and trusted. As a paragon of ethical behaviour Mitra supports and regulates all authorities, the foremost among them being the Sun. Over the centuries, Mitra eventually becomes an associate and representative of the Sun as Sūrya the heavenly body, the luminous and numinous star. Mitra is also the associate of Savitr̥ who is the glorified *principle* or *attribute* of the Sun as a God, enlightener, stimulator and vivifier of all life on Earth. The dual Mitra-Varuṇau is a guarantee of respect and maintenance of order, law, eternity as manifested by the celestial bodies and their movements. Mitra is ever present when serious and important state matters are dealt with.

Varuṇa is unbound but holds in his hands and can use the *pāśa* to chastise and whip the transgressor of the Law and all wicked persons who have been condemned as such. Because of his whip and of the use that Varuṇa makes of it, several authors ancient and modern have erroneously described Varuṇa as a cruel and blood-thirsty deity.

Mitra may be seen also as the *alter ego* of Varuṇa because the pair works in unison. Both these gods are frequently invoked as *kings*, which is correct because besides being gods, they are also rulers who teach the laws and watch over the maintenance of natural order in the world and in the universe. Both Varuṇa and Mitra are also gods because of their glory, their splendour, their perpetual immanence, their might and greatness beyond description. Varuṇa and Mitra, the great gods, are also called kṣatriyas (rulers) in *R̥gveda* VIII. 25, in *R̥gveda* VIII. 67 and elsewhere. All Ādityas are called kṣatriyas, meaning powerful, noble, responsible, calling for obedience and obeisance, responsible for "Order" and "Law". The Laws of Mitra regulate the course of the Sun and we find Mitra at sunrise and Varuṇa at sunset (*AV* XIII. 3.13). Mitra and man learned the laws of *r̥ta* from the Sun who in turn regulates all on Earth and is the greatest Splendour that ancient man could see or imagine. Briefly Mitra and Varuṇa are Lords of Nature and natural order, the first, Mitra is finite in time and space, the second, Varuṇa is eternal but not infinite because there are borders to his "jurisdiction" and limitations to his acts. During his lifetime man often finds himself in painful and distracting situations that Jung (2006: 388, etc.) describes as "conflict of duties" and that I have called elsewhere: "loyalties in conflict." The dual Mitra-Varuṇau indicates how similar situations may cause much mental disorder and how the association of the two powers can help to conquer psychic difficulties. There are facts and situations that are beyond the power of man to control. Paraphrasing from Jung (loc. cit.): "Moral itself means to make a choice between good and bad . . . and there is a moral code that tells us precisely what is "good" or "bad" . . . however present-day individuals are unconscious to such a level as they ignore their faculty or capacity to take a decision." Thus we come back to the ancient dictate: *gnosce te ipsum* (know yourself), which is what Mitra-Varuṇau teach us. The brilliance and importance of the dual Mitra-Varuṇau in the daily life of each one of us, is evident. Man must be prepared to take decisions at every step in life, and they are mostly very hard to take. Indecision and pusillanimous behaviour are often more dangerous even than wrong decisions that could eventually be reverted.

I quote from Jung's autobiography (*Erinnerungen, Traume, Gedanken von Carl Gustav Jung* (tr. mine from it, ed. 1998, G. Russo, p. 388).

> *Nothing can spare us from the acute pain of having to take a moral decision. Under certain situations we must have the freedom . . . to put aside the known reputed standardised moral code and take instead what could be considered to be the wrong decision, if this is what the moral code demands and what we have decided. . . . In other words, we must not bow low to either of the two conflicting decisions. . . . An example is given by the "neti-neti" of Indian philosophy. Under certain conditions the moral code must be abrogated and the individual must take a personal decision. . . . Similar situations are known . . . and are called "conflicting duties".*

In Latin we would say: *in medio est virtus,* meaning that nothing is ever 100 per cent this or that and "virtue" or correct action and behaviour lie in the middle. This is where God Mitra comes to our aid by leaving to our conscience what decision to take in each particular case and which is the least damaging. Whenever there are loyalties in conflict there cannot be a single totally correct answer, but if we would have listened to the teachings and examples given by Mitra, we can reach the best compromise. A classical example comes from the *Rāmāyaṇa*. Prince Rāma takes an immoral decision by shooting an arrow at Bāli (Vāli) from under cover of a tree; however, that was the right decision because at that moment the most important loyalty of the prince was to save his wife Sītā who had been kidnapped. Many years later Rāma, now a king in his own right, is forced to decide against his loyalty and love for Sītā, because a washerman had criticised him for taking back his wife who had spent a long time in captivity of Rāvaṇa, a bad character. King Rāma is now compelled to follow a higher level of loyalty and he must take the most painful decision of sending Sītā in exile which is forced on him by the responsibility that a king has towards the respect and welfare of his people and of his kingdom. The yardstick was weighted differently under different circumstances. Throughout life we have over and over again to take moral decisions, big and small and this is when Mitra, the god of correct measures and proportions comes to help and guides us. The *dexterarum conjunctio*, the hand-clasp of the followers of God Mitra is not only a gesture, it has a meaning deep within us as a mute code of correct moral behaviour if we would only care to listen and be strengthened by it.

With time the personality of Mitra becomes more and more intimately related to Varuṇa though there never is a complete fusion of the two powers, their fields of action or *timai,* are kept carefully independent from each other. Finally Mitra evolves into having the competence, ethical power and correct behaviour that make him guardian of the Cosmic Law that is obvious and manifest as Sūrya the Sun-god, the astral body giver of light and warmth. Mitra/Mythra does not disappear with historical time, as has mistakenly been stated. With time Mitra evolves, becomes differentiated and specialised into several personalities or "gods" created mentally and emotionally by man as Man himself gradually acquires more practical and scientific knowledge and hopefully, also more wisdom, a process usually known as "acculturation." Great and Powerful God Mitra, the guardian of Law and Justice survives and is worshipped and revered from ancient times down to present even if under a variety of names.

Originally there were seven Ādityas: Varuṇa, Mitra, Bhaga, Aryamān, Dakṣa, Aṁśa, and finally Indra the famous leader of the moving clans of the Aryas and most probably an euhemeristic deity (Chakravarty, 1997). The number of Ādityas later increased to 12 according to various traditions. To these was later added Mārtaṇḍa, another name for Sūrya (Bhargava, 2001).

Among the Ādityas one of the most frequently mentioned, revered and invoked together or after Mitra, is Bhaga the divider who allocates the portion or role and part that life has in store for each and everyone of us. As a synonym of words such as Lord, Blessed, Wise, Glorious, Divine, Saint, Venerable and others, Bhaga is at present usually addressed as Bhagavān. The Vedic Bhaga becomes *Baga* or *Baya* (lord, powerful and rich, meaning also: a portion, a part of . . .) in the *Avesta*. In Slavonic languages the general word for god is still *Bog*. In Avestic, Bhaga is written *Baga*.

Bhaga and all the Ādityas are haters of falsehood, they punish sin and protect their worshippers by tying up their enemies with fetters. Mitra is called *king* in the only hymn addressed exclusively to Mitra alone (*Ṛgveda* III. 59). Mitra is otherwise associated mainly to Varuṇa and in *Ṛgveda* VIII. 25, 4 both Mitra and Varuṇa are called *deva, samrāja* (universal kings) and *asura*. These words mean great, mighty, powerful, unusually gifted with exceptional intelligence and prophetical acumen. The Vedic Aryans were *asura* worshippers because these deities were well-wishers and helpful. Only in the latest hymns of the *Ṛgveda*, such as *ṚV*. VI. 22.4 and others (*see* Bhargava loc. cit. for more details and explanations), the word *asura* acquires the meaning of *demon*, meaning a *being* gifted with great power that he often uses maliciously. Bhargava also points out that the schism between the Indo-Aryan and Indo-Iranian clans or tribes occurred towards the end of the Ṛgvedic period when the word *asura* became a synonym of *dānava* and *daitya* among the Indo-Aryans.

In the course of time and in the Purāṇic period the words *dānava* and *daitya* acquired the current meaning of demons.[4]

Bhargava (2001) states convincingly that: "Varuṇa's chief epithets *asura* and *medhira* became the name of the Iranian Supreme God under the form of *Ahura-Mazda.* Indra's well-known epithet *Vṛtrahan* became an independent god under the form *Verethraghna.*" Bhargava also gives numerous other proofs of the early divergent evolution of the twin cultures, the Indo-Aryan and the Indo-Iranian as well as proofs of their close relationship over centuries or millennia of ancient history.

Ṛgveda III. 59 is the only Vedic hymn addressed to Mitra alone. The personality of God Mitra is described, understood, explained, revered, lauded, prayed to with oblations made in the holy fire. The god is loved in all its significance and worth, beginning with its cosmogonic role as Sustainer of the Earth and Heaven. Finally he is invoked for his glory and the hymn closes with the following statement:

> All the five races (of Indo-Aryans) have repaired to Mitra ever strong to aid,
>
> For he sustaineth all the Gods.
>
> Mitra to gods, to living men, to him who strew the holy grass
> Gives food fulfilling the sacred Law
>
> — Ṛṣi Viśvāmitra, tr. Griffith, *ṚV* III. 59.8/9

Mitra is invoked and prayed to in over 175 hymns of the *ṚV*. Most often Mitra is remembered in association with Varuṇa and the two Ādityas are mentioned as a pair, Mitra-Varuṇau. Varuṇa is the only unbound Āditya, he is the dynamic portion of the part of the universe known to man. Varuṇa's domain is limited and contained in the *universe* or *cosmos;* it includes Earth, Sky and Intermediate regions. Unlike Varuṇa, Mitra is bound by fetters, as the other Ādityas are and he is eternal as all the Ādityas are, including Varuṇa. Summing up, Time and Space taken together are a *continuum* that can be *eternal* meaning that it can exist indefinitely in time and space but may eventually come to an end, even if only at a very distant past or future, but only Aditi is *infinite*. In mathematics the Greek letter *phi*, or *golden mean* is the symbol of the Fibonacci number, an irrational number that cannot be written as a finite fraction or an integer (see Livio, 2003). It is possible to go on dividing the numbers that produce the *phi* indefinitely without ever repeating them and never arriving at a rational fraction (=a cardinal number). In Euclidian geometry *phi* is a very special rapport between the whole and its parts. Ciocci, 2003, elaborates on the question of proportionality in nature and art in his most interesting book entitled *Luca Pacioli and the Mathematization of Knowledge in the Renaissance*, that is completed with an exhaustive bibliography on the subject.

It is impossible to imagine a habitable universe without Order. If it ever existed, it would have been the primordial *chaos*, hinted at and imagined by many ancient wise men and religions, including some ancient Indian "seers", the *ṛṣis*. Internal evidence from the Vedas demonstrate that ancient *ṛṣis* saw Varuṇa as the "one who knows" and oversees order in the Universe while Mitra is his executor, hence the constant association of the two. Varuṇa sees reality or Truth with his mind and acts with his *pāśa*s while Mitra ensures obeisance to the Law and maintenance of Order because of his wisdom. With the passage of time, with increasing knowledge and wisdom as well as growing social complexity and differentiation, Mitra becomes diversified and specialised, but not diluted or weakened; he engenders ever new gods as created by cultural development and as diversified into many topics of discussion, care and development. Laws proliferate for the sake of adaptation to changed and evolving practical, ecological, intellectual and social conditions of mankind. Mitra continues to be ever present in his original form and in the garb of new personalities, as required by new discoveries, by the development of technicalities, as well as by growing scientific knowledge. One such is the Mithra of the Mithraea of the Graeco-Roman world that flourished from the last century BCE up to the middle first millennium CE and later.

Varuṇa encompasses, encloses, surrounds, envelops and includes everything that ancient man could see, touch, smell, eat, drink and imagine. Varuṇa is all Nature with its exclusive laws and man who is part of it. Mitra was Varuṇa's *mitra,* the ideal friend, the associate and safeguard who exists in Varuṇa's world. Mitra therefore can be nothing else but a friend of man, puny little man who was originated and lives by the grace of what existed earlier and whose origin and limits he could not himself even attempt to guess. As they appear in the Vedas, Varuṇa and Mitra are the most ancient gods of man when he had already learned how to make and control fire, Agni the first man-made *god* of *Homo habilis* (Vannucci, 1999). They represent the understanding that man had of the Universe's fundamental realities which man gradually expressed as *Truth* and represented as *ṛta.* Mitra is not only guardian of the cosmic laws, he is guardian also of man-made laws, and like Varuṇa, he is also Truth itself with its myriad facets. He surveys the movements and arrays of the people and guides the "five migrating tribes of the Aryas." Mitra is very human and is said to give command also by voice! Would this be an indication that Mitra includes also Sound as music, rhythm and harmony to complete the whole of man's nature and his place in the world?

Varuṇa, Mitra and Savitṛ are the universal laws of this world and of the entire universe. Mitra watches over the solar cycle and Varuṇa takes over in the evening, when the only guiding lights are those of the moon and stars and eventually also the fires made by man. Quoting from Bhargava (loc. cit., p. 334)

> *. . . Mitra is a solar deity and it is corroborated by the Avesta where Mitra is undoubtedly a sun god. . . . Just as the Vedic Mitra is associated to Varuṇa, the Avestic Mithra is also closely associated with Ahura-Mazda, the Iranian successor of Asura Varuṇa.*

We shall think about the *dexiosis* or *dexterarum conjunctio,* the "hand grasp or handshake" between Mitra and Sūrya and of man and man further on. Mitra, a paragon of ethical behaviour, is also a leader and king to whom the five initial Indo-European clans yield submission, he "marshals men by uttering his voice . . . and the epithet *yātayajjana* = arraying men together is peculiarly his. Savitṛ is said to become Mitra because of his laws, and Viṣṇu is said to make his three steps by the laws of Mitra" (*ṚV* VIII.52.3). These and other statements also indicate that Mitra (wise, wise measures, wise movements, correct proportions) regulates the course of Sūrya the heavenly body who in turn reports back to Mitra: a punctiliously, mathematically regulated feedback mechanism. Mitra was prepared to enter Rome as a military god.

The name Varuṇa could be derived from the ancient Indo-European root-word *wa* that may be read as "void," Latin *vā* and *va,* in this case "the great universe." It could also be derived from *wat* = prophetic, oracular, akin to Latin *vates* that occurs in similar forms in Germanic and Celtic languages. Varuṇa and Mitra are divine and prophetic because of their antiquity (*medhira),* (*ṚV* III.25.20) and their exactitude. Mitra was engendered or begotten by Aditi specifically to become the law maker and Judge Supreme. Thus the Mitra-Varuṇau pair, where each is bound to the other by their original nature and by a pact consecrated by the *dexiosis,* is the Spirit and Power that knows the rules of Order and can advise and regulate individuals, populations and nations.[5]

As the eternal associate of Varuṇa the Lord who reigns supreme, Mitra is Splendour itself. Mitra, bound by strings is associated to Sūrya-Savitṛ the main solar deity who sees everything that is and happens on Earth, similarly as Ahura-Mazda who is the supreme god of Mazdeism. The many new gods who were facets of the original Mitra-Mithra with time became themselves characterised and endowed with different aspects of light, honesty, cleanliness, as well as of freedom of behaviour with total responsibility of every human individual's own thoughts and actions and their consequences. Using contemporary terms the best words to describe Mitra, even if incompletely, could be: dispenser of Justice, embodiment of understanding and sympathy, as well as: the physical-chemical-biological sense of affinity, amity, similarity, alliance and above all, fusion and integration, responsibility, manliness and generosity, but definitely not petty piety for piety's sake. Mitra is a genuine archetype in Jung's terminology and he should better be remembered at present more than ever before.

As a virtual but well-defined personality Mitra survives to this day and his name is used in Hindi, Urdu, and other Indian languages that I do not know, to designate a very special and true friend and personal counsellor — a friend always ready to give moral support and serenity of mind because of one's own accomplished duty and responsible behaviour. Mitra is the immanence of cosmic order and function and therefore of Truth, Essence and Reality. In terms of Advaita Vedānta we may represent mentally the personality of Mitra throughout his long and continuing existence as one of the "possibilities" or "qualifications" of *Saguṇa Brahman* that may vary according to circumstances, times and personalities.[6]

5

The Indo-Iranian / Persian God Mithra / Mithraism

The Most Ancient Past

ALL the most ancient Indo-European people who called themselves *Arya* (Skt. lord, noble) and moved into Central Asia at different periods and various migratory waves were mostly nomads and shared the same basic language and culture. Those with a recorded history are better known to us, they are the Indo-Aryans (Indo-Aryan) who eventually settled in the geographic region that is now called India or Major India, and the Indo-Iranians (Indo-Iranian) who settled in the region now called Iran and nearby geographic areas of Central Asia. Among the latter those more closely related to the Indo-Aryan lived in Sogdiana and Chorasmia (Khwarizm), in northern Iran. Sogdiana, in the *doab* between the Amu Daryā and the Syr Daryā played a significant role in the building of Iran/Persia. Both these areas were and remained for millennia the historical nodal area linking diverse Asian regions among them (Vannucci, 2007, forthcoming). Because of this their role in the troubled evolution of their culture over the centuries is particularly interesting. There is a large amount of records of the Aryas, both I-I and I-A that range from palaeontology to written documents, from mythology to surviving traditions, from the oral tradition to technical, mathematical, empirical and scientific knowledge, as well as phonetic, artistic and musical heritage that have come down to us. Carl Gustav Jung (1875-1961) refers often to the traditional Indian wisdom and practical knowledge, specially when he discusses the role of "archetypes" in the functioning of the human mind and mental balance.[7]

The Indo-Iranian and Indo-Aryan shared the same cultural substrate and the same original theogony and theology. The social structure of these two groups was the same, their religion and habits were comparable. They had initially domesticated the same plants and animals, had invented and used the wheel and had a special attachment for the horse that had first been bred for meat but had later become an essential associate of man for transport, riding, fighting or hunting from horseback. At a later stage, the Indo-Iranian also domesticated the two-humped camel better suited than the single hump camel (*Camelus dromedarius*) of the Indo-Aryan for work in cold and dry regions. There are numerous reliefs and carvings of the two-humped camel (popularly known as Bactrian camel) at Persepolis. Well developed irrigation systems appropriate for the geographic area between and beyond the river system of the Amu Daryā and Syr Daryā were very advanced already in the first half of the last millennium BCE and earlier.

At some yet unidentified time the early stages of cultural development the Indo-Aryan and of the Indo-Iranian evolved along divergent directions. This change was mainly due to the different environments where these two branches of Indo-Europeans (I-E) moved through and eventually settled in. The most important single ecological factor that determined movements and settlements was the year-round or alternately seasonal availability of water, hence the secure association of God Varuṇa with water, including the seas while Mitra, the god of measures and proportions became a close associate of Sūrya, the Sun God and of Savitṛ. The composite name Ahura-Mazda consecrates the symbiosis between the forces that create and make life possible on Earth, namely Solar energy and Water. Solar energy is the essential requirement for the photosynthetic process to take place. Without solar energy there would be no higher form of Life on Earth and solar energy is also the driving force that moves waters and the recycling of water by evaporation as vapour, precipitation as rain or snow and drainage of surface or underground liquid water. Ancient man was well aware that water and warmth were the two indispensable factors for the creation and maintenance of life on Earth. Varuṇa and the inseparable fusion Ahura-Mazda remain forever the Great God identified with Splendour, Brightness and Life remembered and consecrated by Mazdeism. In Vedism the association Mitra-Varuṇau regulates in measured proportions the factors that ensure living and becomes in pre-Zarathustra Avestism, the association between Mithra and Ahura (Varuṇa)-Mazda (Splendour) which is Ahura-Mazda (Might and Splendour). In Vedism the indelible association of the two great Gods Mitra and Varuṇa is expressed repeatedly and amongst others it is celebrated also in the Gāyatrī *mantra* (*R̥gveda* III. 62.10). The *dexiosis,* the hand clasp of Sūrya, the Sun God with Mitra, the Great God of Justice symbolises the eternal association and correspondence that ensure the perpetuation of Life on Earth. The *dexiosis* or *dexterarum conjunctio* is represented in one or other way in all Mythraea.

Mitra is the personification of the concept of measures and proportions, while the Sun/Sūrya/Savitr̥ is the manifestation of divine force, power and energy. Nevertheless historical Mitra over time changed robes but not roles or meaning, according to the ecological, historical and political demands made on him by Man, but his fundamental *timai*: the god's duties, his competence, his field of action; his jurisdiction remained eternally unchanged: the maintenance of order in the cosmos.

Mitra (=Mithra) is seldom represented in the Indo-Aryan iconography and mostly so only in late BCE and early CE periods. Mithra is the central figure shown in the Mithraea and during the period of dominance of the Mithraic religion. There are no figures of Mitra that I know of from early Vedic times, when there was no iconography anyhow, up to the second half of the last millennium BCE when god Mithra appears in the I-I/Persian figurative arts. With the development of Mithraism, Mithra becomes the central figure of the Mithraea where the god is represented in sculptures in low and high relief or in the round, as well as on paintings, mosaics, cloth, symbolically and otherwise. In the Roman period, late last century BCE to *c.* fifth century CE, the most frequent representations of Mithra are the tauroctony or killing of the bull, and the *dexiosis* or *dexterarum conjunctio.*[8]

The Indo-Aryan movements were oriented towards abundant running waters, to the legendary "land of the seven rivers, Saptasindhava," the entire Indus River system already known to earlier ancient Asian cultures. Similarly the Indo-Iranians were also guided by the need of perennial water supply. This they found in the northern regions of the twin rivers Amu Daryā and Syr Daryā that flow into the Aral Sea. Later the Indo-Iranians occupied also the ancient land of Elam in south-western Iran, which was named Parsa (=Phars, Fars) after the new arrivals (Ghirshman, 1977) and was irrigated by the Tigris/Euphrates River system. They inherited from earlier cultures water management practices that they improved and extended further over large geographic areas to allow for the growth of urbanisation.

All the lands where the Indo-Iranians settled were known to be rich areas. The lands of northern present-day Iran included what was later called by the Romans Margiana, Bactria, Parthia, Chorasmia (=Khwarizm) and Sogdiana, the latter (or more probably the border area with Chorasmia) is the reputed birthplace of Zarathustra who lived and preached under the patronage of the local king Vistaspa (*aśva, aspa*=horse) a typical I-A name of one or several kings mentioned also in the genealogies and elsewhere in the Indian Purāṇas. Other groups of I-I and other I-E people, important among them the Medes, also moved into Central Asia coming from the geographic area beyond the Caucasus mountains. This western branch of the Indo-Iranian (see Ghirsman, 1977; Vannucci, 2007, forthcoming) met non-I-E people in Central and South Asia, important among them the Elamites, the Sumerians, and most probably also Draviḍians. The fusion of the Indo-Iranians with other ancient people who had developed sophisticated, extensive and long-lasting engineering works mainly to save, store and use water rationally on a sustainable basis, contributed further to the acculturation of the Central Asia populations. Enhanced personal, agricultural, urban and social development were directly influenced and adapted to climates and other environmental parameters such as geological formations and above all to the seasonal availability of waters above and below ground (see Laureano, 1993, 1998, 2001, 2002). Laureano gives many examples of man's practicality applied to living conditions in inhospitable regions with prevailing water restrictions.

The I-A culture finally evolved mainly towards an agricultural simple way of life in water rich areas and monsoon dominated climates. Both Indo-Iranians and Indo-Aryans used and developed hydrological works appropriate for different environmental conditions, from high mountain ranges to major river valleys west and east of the Indus River system. They also improved, developed and extended further over great distances an impressive web of roads and communication systems, including river transport that had already been sketched, planned and used by their predecessors. These and others are among the innumerable examples of man's ingenuity to respond to the pressures of ecological determinants on the evolution of cultures, including religions.

The significant point for the subject matter of this concise essay is that the most ancient gods of the I-A and I-I are and were the same but they eventually evolved along divergent paths due to the different environments in the areas where the various groups settled or where they continued to roam about. Cultural exchanges and political-martial pressures of other people of the same or different origin (Liverani et al., 2009) also contributed to push development along different paths. The ancient-most gods of all these people who called themselves Arya and shared the same basic language are easily recognisable even when and where we find variants in the names or attributes of the gods themselves. There is no doubt that the original religion/ philosophy of the Indo-Iranians and of the I-A was based on the ecological parameters of the physical world where they lived. In other words, the common to all religion was based on the environmental realities and laws of Nature, both material and mental. However, beyond and above the basic common culture and religion, something happened that caused a schism between the twin cultures, the I-A and I-I.

Many hypotheses about the schism were offered by scholars, but no consensus has been reached. I postulate here that the schism that divided the two groups and created a chasm that was never filled was, amongst others, caused by the imposing figure of Zarathustra who cursed the "*daeva* worshippers" meaning the I-A. Zarathustra declared them enemies forever. Where and exactly when this happened, is another question that will not be addressed here. We know that the Indo-Aryans migrated towards Central Asia probably as early as two millennia before the Indo-Iranians moved in the same general direction, coming from the Eurasian steppes north of the Caspian and Aral seas. It seems reasonable to hypothesise that when the I-I arrived in the region that is now northern Iran, they found that the I-A culture had drifted away from its origins and that the cultural gap between the two groups could not be reversed. The gap would better be marked and characterised by new religious injunctions and this could have happened because of Zarathurtra's teachings, *c.* sixth century BCE. The Vedic gods

Mitra and Varuṇa of the Avestic pre-Zarathustra period were consecrated by the prophet as the two "immortal benefactors," living and acting under Ahura (Varuṇa)-Mazda, the mighty and highest God, the overseer of men taken individually and collectively. Ahura-Mazda was thereafter revered as the Only Supreme Wise God by the Iranians and Persians. The profound meanings of words such as Asura (Ahura) and compound or derivate words are best understood when seen from the same perspective and full meaning of the Greek word *daimon*: any supernatural Being or Power endowed with great force that the *daimon* itself may use for good or bad.

Mazdeism was the established religion throughout the Achaemenid period and following centuries. Later Mazdeism was weakened or disappeared gradually with the establishment of Christianity in the West, including much of the Mediterranean world and Central Asia, and more so later, with the advent of Islam in Asia. In India Vedism evolved into Brāhmanism and Hinduism among others, and the religions that followed them.

The most ancient gods of the I-A and the I-I were the same. Specially meaningful for the present study is the presence of Mitra, or Mithra, as the name is spelled in Pahlavī and of Varuṇa, known in Iran/Persia as Ahura that is the Iranian pronunciation of Varuṇa, as clearly explained by Bhargava (2001).[9] Religions, philosophies and habits diverged when these two populations who were already living in Central Asia, migrated in opposite directions and became adapted to new environments, including other people and diverse cultures. On this matter I should again refer to Bhargava (2001: 47-70) who gives a clear and complete documented explanation of the evolution of the two cultures, of the etymology of names and of the development of the personalities of gods and deities, as well as of their attributes or *timai*. Bhargava points out:

> *. . . Thus, if we examine the conception of gods alone we find that the Ṛgvedic gods underwent four main types of changes in the*

> *Purāṇas as well as in the Avesta. . . . The fourth change . . . both in the Avesta and in the Purāṇas is with regard to those R̥gvedic gods who on account of their popularity stood in the way of pure monotheism or the worship of God under one definite name.*

This was the position up to the first half of the last millennium BCE when the situation changed with the advent of Zarathustra (Zarthosht; Zoroaster) who convinced himself and others that he could converse, listen and talk to the Supreme Wise Lord Ahura-Mazda "who can create just with his thought" and who is the impersonal essence of all that is good. The I-A maintained their ancient faith in nature and nature gods and because of this the I-A are called and condemned as *daeva* worshippers in the *Avesta* and other Indo-Iranian texts. Among the I-I Varuṇa becomes Ahura, intimately associated to the Great Might and Light of Mazda.

Zarathustra lived and preached under the patronage of King Vistaspa. Zarathustra preached that people individually and collectively should be faithful followers of Ahura-Mazda's teachings and should persistently deny and condemn the "demoniac" (from Lt. *daemon*, Greek *daimon*, a Socratic word/concept = a divine power, might, energy) followers of the mistaken gods of the *daeva*, meaning the Indo-Aryans who had remained strict adherents of the original naturalistic religion. The ancient-most gods common to all the I-A and I-I were the "powers" (spirits, entities), unimaginable and non-describable creators who could be known best or exclusively from their attributes and manifestations such as Agni, god of Fire, the most important of them. Among these mental representations of the divine power, Aditi, not mentioned under this name in the *Avesta*, as we now have it, is the Universal Mother, one of the most meaningful, realistic and powerful figures of the original and perhaps primordial pantheon of all the clans of I-E who migrated into Central Asia at different times and periods. Aditi, Mother of all, is one of the ancient-most archetypes. She represents the concept of Infinite or Infinity. She engendered seven "sons". Everyone of the seven except Varuṇa (=Ahura in the *Avesta*) were restrained by imaginary *pāśas* (fetters, strings, ties, limitations). Varuṇa (the one who encompasses everything) is the only unfettered son of Aditi and he is said "to enclose the whole world." We can understand Varuṇa as the concept of "eternal". Mitra was the next in line of "spiritual powers" ("sons" of Aditi), he was restrained by strings (fetters, constraints) as all the other Ādityas and all men are, except Varuṇa. Varuṇa's role in the world was to supervise and teach the Order and Law of the Universe and inflict punishment on transgressors of the Law following the verdicts passed by Mitra, the Great Judge who sits on the Cinvat Bridge that separates the world of the living from that of the deceased. The judgements passed by Mitra are circumscribed by the "limitations, dictates and realities" defined by Aditi who is herself the Universe, the idea of "*Infinite*".[10]

Varuṇa is the first and the only "son" of Aditi who is not restrained by ties or fetters because he is eternal though not infinite as Aditi. Varuṇa knows and governs the ethical behaviour of man and other elements of the world known to man (*see* chapters 3 and 4). Some authors ancient and modern describe Varuṇa (Ahura) as a fierce, cruel, vindictive god who uses his whip to punish and destroy his enemies. The word "his enemies" is a mistake since wrong-doers and sinners are not Varuṇa's enemies, they are indeed man's enemies. The second mistake is to consider Varuṇa to be a cruel god; actually Varuṇa does not use the whip because of his own preference or moved by cruel instincts but because he is the executor of the verdicts passed by the Great Judge Mitra who sits on the Cinvat Bridge. Varuṇa uses the whip for the sake of maintenance of order in the universe, he uses his fetters as a whip because it is his duty, his *timai* according to the realities of Aditi, the Universe, and not because he is vicious and bad.

The dual Mitra/Varuṇau has survived for centuries and is

historically manifest *mutatis mutandis* for worse and with appropriate adaptations in the dark episodes of the Inquisition of the Roman Catholic Church and other dictatorships. On the other hand, we may look at the pragmatism of the Anglo-Saxon mind and the long-lasting fidelity to Authority and to the king and other rulers as a "left-over" memory or as the manifestation of a collective archetype that survives from the teachings of Mithraism: absolute fidelity to the state, king, empire and system.

Lévi Sylvain in *La Dottrina del sacrificio nei Brahmana* (2009) discusses the personality of Varuṇa and represents the God as a relentless punisher of incorrect behaviour because Varuṇa's function is to be the guarantor and executor of the Law. In addition to the fetters that he carries he is also the god of all waters, stagnant, fresh or running waters, because Water is a synonym of cleanliness and purity (*Maitra Saṁ*. II.5.6). Mitra and Varuṇa, the dual Mitra-Varuṇau is a specially consecrated pair and we find water in all Mithraea of the Roman period, where clever hydrological works ensure abundant running water and storage. It is impossible to have Life without water.

The image of the two gods or the duo Mitra/Varuṇa as visualised in Vedism and Brāhmanism, and discussed in the *Śatapatha Brāhmaṇa* or in the *Maitrāyaṇīya Upaniṣad* and throughout the most ancient sacred texts, is one of perfect accuracy, reality, fidelity, honesty, knowledge, justice, wisdom in man's mind, it is the embodiment of never failing Trust and Truth. This image is also the image of Ahura-Mazda as incorporated in Mithraism. Water is the materialisation, if I may say so, of the personality of Varuṇa that evolved from Vedism/Avestism, through Mazdeism and Zoroastrianism to full-fledged Mithraism and beyond. "Varuṇa of the thousand waters, of running waters is Life, he is the Saviour of existence, truth, reality and faith . . . everything that exists takes rest, even the wind may take rest but waters never rest (*Śat*. III.9.2.5) and (*Maitra*, IV.5.4) . . . Waters provide peace and serenity." This symbolism lived and was carried over materially also in the Roman Mithraea where running water and fresh water pots were always at hand. The importance and role of water wherever, is shared in some way or other by all cultures and religions. Varuṇa is everywhere revered under its many forms and myriad names. In late Hinduism Varuṇa is present as the powerful God of all waters, including the sea. Everlasting Varuṇa is the reality of existence, of *ṛta* and of life as we know it. The dual Mitra-Varuṇau shares with man the eagerness to participate in the cosmic drama and as a faith and culture it addresses the practicalities of life on earth. It has survived for centuries and evolved, *mutatis mutandis* for instance in the pragmatism of the English people and language. Mithraism could not take a lasting foothold in the Mediterranean and other parts of the world where earlier cultures and faiths had already taken root and had occupied a large portion of the cultural habits and customs of the people, leaving only restricted space for a newly introduced cult.

Evolution of the Personality of Mitra/Mithra

From the early Mitra of the nomads, through the age of Mitra of the great pastures, the God eventually grew to be the military god of the great powers, but in the heart of the Mithraea the ancient rituals were still celebrated for the initiation and indoctrination of all the postulants and catechumens, for the salvation of Man and of Mother Earth, for the mutual assistance and resilience of members of the community and for the illusion of Empire and its Emperors during the last century BCE and through the age of the hegemony of Rome and later. The *dexterarum conjunctio* or "conjunction of the right hands," the sacred pact of devoted friendship, even if rarely remembered in its full meaning, survives to this day, also in India, Italy, places in Europe and elsewhere as a promise, an act of faith in each other. How would it be possible to survive without Faith? It is meaningful that Mithraism talks of "conjunction," but not "fusion": the association of Mitra with Sūrya/Savitṛ and of Mitra, Mithra or Mythra with Ahura-Mazda is a deliberate and most powerful bond that can be eternal but that could even break down. As in fact it occasionally did or does because of political changes over time and above all because of the frailty and fickleness of the human mind (*ṚV* X. 86, Indra and Vṛṣakapi).

Most frequently in the *dexterarum conjunctio* or *dexiosis*, the handshake of Mithra with the Sun God, Savitṛ for the Indo-Aryan and with Ahura-Mazda for the Indo-Iranian, Mitra represents knowledge, wisdom, law and justice and the Sun represents and incorporates life in all its positive aspects. The *dexiosis* has a much more profound and lasting meaning than the kiss, both Judas' and the repetitive, superficial, modern, cheap kisses blown astray by fashion and winds.[10]

The Early Ṛgvedic and Avestic periods are represented by the *gāthā* (songs) that are "hymns" in an I-E language very close and essentially similar to archaic Sanskrit, perhaps with a different pronunciation and intonation of the phonemes. The *gāthā* of the Indo-Iranian and Indo-Aryan early periods are not contemporaneous and are not alike in content, but they are comparable in the sense of Jung's (2006,) words: ". . . Myths are the very first form of science" and ". . . myths die if they stop living and developing." One of the basic characteristics of Hinduism is its vitality and continuous growth and versatility that keep the religion in tune with cultural evolution over time and with the interpretation and re-interpretations needed to maintain alive and functional the eternal truths of the various philosophical schools. Myths are very much alive in the Vedic lore down to present, as much as sound in general and music in particular. They have been a powerful element in the process of acculturation and education of all people and Indian people in particular. Among them music and rhythm played a role comparable to the invention and use of script in other civilisations. Śiva Naṭarāja, Lord of the Cosmic Tāṇḍava Dance that put the world in motion is the *oṁkāra*, the *oṁ* (*auṁ*) the sacred immortal syllable, the *akṣara* (sound, letter, syllable) that includes all sounds, including silence that is the absence of sound and engulfs in itself the concept of *ātman*, pure all-pervading Conscience and the symbol of the Absolute *Brahman*.

The awareness of the rhythmic heartbeat exists in our inner self since before birth and has been used as a measure of time consciously and subconsciously by everybody, as well as a measure of the emotional state of the person at any particular moment. Music as harmony and melody is a measure and combination of sounds that produces effective feelings of pleasure, love, pain or other emotions opposed to those caused by cacophonies. Ancient languages like Sanskrit that has survived the test of time, is pure music when well pronounced, to the point that putting spoken language in writing form was for centuries considered in India and among other reasons, to be a superfluous exercise. God Mitra, the measure of time and space exists since the "beginning of Time" and because Mitr (*sic*) is "measure" he was first put in writing as simple arithmetic. In this sense the ancient Vedic Sacrifices have a scope in themselves, and this is the tuning of the inner I with the "music of the spheres" or Perfection, we could preferably say, with "The Absolute Truth", *Brahman*. The Vedic Sacrifice is meant to be the practice and support that helps man to participate in the cosmic drama and thus "absorb" Reality into his inner self. Music like mathematics is perceived by the sense organs and is engraved in the inner Self thanks to the functioning of the living brain. Sound and music in general do not produce readily recognisable archaeological remains but may survive somehow as archetypes inbuilt in the individual and collective Self as music and rhythm.

God Mitra, along with other Vedic Gods, is historically known and named as one of the Hittite gods who presided over the sealing of the Treaty agreed upon by Pharaoh Ramses II of Egypt and King Muwatalli II of Hatti (Hattusha) a few years after the Battle of Qadesh. The Treaty was sealed by the two parties in *c.* 1270/1275 BCE about seven centuries before the birth of Zarathustra, it was written and copied in more than one script, including cuneiform adapted to the language spoken by the Hittites, a form of ancient Sanskrit with inclusions of Hurrite vocabulary. The text of the treaty was reproduced also in hieroglyphs and in cursive Egyptian and various languages and other scripts for political purposes. The Gods invoked by the Hittites to sanction the treaty were the most ancient Indo-Aryan gods, namely Mitra, Varuṇa, Indra and the Nāsatyas (Twins). Local gods of the Hurrite people who formed the bulk of the populations of the Hittite kingdom and of Mitanni, are also invoked and mentioned as additional witnesses to legalise the Treaty for posterity. The most important among the local gods was the great and powerful Lord of Tempests. The Treaty and the copious correspondence exchanged between the rulers and matchmakers of both sides (Vannucci, 2007, and forthcoming) before and after the sealing of the Treaty are dated and provide firm benchmarks that underline the evolution and development in place and time of the personality of God Mitra (Mythra) and other gods and deities in the pre-Zarathustra Age. (*figs* 1 and 2).

It is thus historically proved that God Mitra was already an "ancient traditional god" with the authority to witness and legalise the Pact drawn between the two powers, the Hittite and the Egyptian long before the advent of Zarathustra. As a matter of fact, both the parties honoured the accord agreed upon and sealed with the Treaty, peace reigned between them and in the entire region for a period of about two centuries. The Annals of the Hittite kingdom had been and continued to be systematically recorded on bronze tablets since the early second millennium BCE and besides the text of the Treaty, they include also the Acts and a large number of letters exchanged between the Great Prince (king) Suppiluliuma I of Hatti (Hattusha), middle fourteenth century BCE (Guidotti and Daddi, 2002) and other kings and people of his time. The rich correspondence exchanged between King Suppiluliuma I and his son Mursili II of Hatti with the pharaohs of that period were referred to and/or translated recently by several scholars. To mention a few: Edel, E. Korrespondenz, *Die aegyptisch-hethitische Korrespondenz aus Boghazkoi in babylonischer und hethitischer Sprache*, vols. 1, 2; Guidotti and Daddi (2002, 1, 2, publ. *Museo Archeologico Nazionale*); M. Liverani (1988), *Antico oriente. Storia, società . . . , economia, Gius.* Laterza and Figli, Spa. Roma-Bari; Liverani, *M. Le lettere di el-Amarna*, vols. 1-2, Brescia 1908; G.F. del Monte (1993); Moran (1987) and others.

Figs. 1 and 2 in this essay show the imprint of two seals of Suppiluliuma I of Hattusha (fourteenth century BCE). What appears to be and has been correctly interpreted as the solar disc is shown above a saddle-shaped support provided with a long waving wing on either side. The "saddle" or "throne" is in turn placed over a design that, if compared with *fig*. 3 in this essay, reminds the "necklace [more probably a belt clasp]" shown in *fig*. 5 from Dandamayev (1996). The clasp is of the same style and is made of gold like numerous other objects of the collections of the "Hermitage" in St Petersburg (Russia) in *fig*. 4 that are also made of pure gold and are beautifully worked and chiselled by Scythian (Saka) goldsmiths. The emblem shown on this clasp is the same as the stereotype symbol of Ahura-Mazda widely reproduced on carvings, seals and prints of the Achaemenid period (second half of the first millennium BCE). *Figs*. 5, 6 show Ahura-Mazda to be the same personality represented on the seal of Suppiluliuma I cast eight to nine centuries earlier as mentioned above. *Fig*. 6 shows Ahura-Mazda on horseback, with both the god and the head of his horse looking westwards. The God is on horseback but the hanging side-panel of his robe partially hides the details of the harness. There is even a slight attempt at perspective with the left wing seen on a back plane.

There is no doubt that the God of Hittite king Suppiluliuma of Hatti (Hattusha) of the fourteenth centuruy BCE is the Supreme

Good God Ormazd (Mazda), twin brother of the Bad God Ahriman of pre-Zoroastrian Avestism.

Going back in time we may conclude that there are firm dates for the earliest "invasion", or better described, the gradual "infiltration" of the I-A in Asia Minor. It was a long process running over an unspecified period of one or more centuries. The timing is the early centuries of the second millennium BCE. The people on the move would need a powerful and determined leader to co-ordinate the movements and ensure firm settling in the chosen new territories. This warrior leader may be easily identified with Indra and his followers the Maruts who were originally storm gods in the *R̥gveda*. Evidently the I-A nomads coming at different times and probably in rather small groups needed a protective escort of mounted men. These agree very well with the repeated descriptions of the *rudrasya maryaḥ* who are present in both the oral and the written tradition as young mounted warriors faithful to Indra, they introduced the horse and the chariot in West Central Asia. Chakravarty (1997) argues convincingly about the euhemeristic nature of God Indra and of his faithful Maruts.

There are proved dates for the reigns of Hattusili I and Mursili I in northern Mesopotamia around the seventeenth century BCE when King Hattusili had a firm standing on the Hittite throne at Hattusha and was well informed on technological innovations. King Hattusili had better use of trained horsepower and a well-organised system of governance based on a web of well-defined alliances and pacts, reinforced by oaths rooted in the principle of faithfulness, in which we can see clearly the presence of God Mitra who eventually and much later in Rome justifies a rigorous military organisation, including the use of the trumpet in war and peace. The first widely applied and documented fruits of the system were reaped at, and following the inconclusive Battle of Qadesh (1275 BCE).

There is no doubt that the Vedic and the Hittite God Mitra

are one and the same, they are also the same as pre- and post-Zarathustra God Mithra who is invoked and eulogised throughout the *Avesta*. There is no doubt that the pre- and post-Zarathustra Supreme Spirit Ahura-Mazda is likewise one and the same Entity. There is also no doubt that the Avestan Mitra is the same as the Vedic Mitra who is the same as the late Iranian/ Persian Mithra and God of the Roman Mithraea.

Just a few quotes: *Yn.* 1.3 eulogises Mithra as "the [lord] of the ample pastures, with thousand ears and countless (myriad) eyes, he is the *yazata* (venerable, spirit; from *yaz* = to honour, to venerate) whose name was revered along with that of *Rāman Hvāstra* (the *yazata* of joy, air, peace and good pastures (*Yn.* 1.3; *Yn.* 68.15, etc.). The Avestic Mithra (Pahlavī *miihr, mihir* = shining, brilliant, luminous) (Lt = splendorous, transcendent), presides over agreements, treatises and judgements; he is the surveyor of the fulfilment of the Law of Justice and Order. The *dexiosis* of Mithra and Sūrya (Sun, Savitr̥, Ahura-Mazda), originally called *dexterarum cojunctio* or "right-hand clasp" was the correct gesture for mutual identification and recognition among the followers of Mithraism. It is repeatedly shown in reliefs, paintings, mosaics throughout the Roman Empire and elsewhere.

The figure of the *dexiosis* was a development and evolution of the winged image of Ahura-Mazda himself. The iconography of the symbols of Ahura-Mazda and of the *dexiosis* (here *fig.* 8, from Ossanna, 1998, *see* cover) are comparable in concept, placement and intention. The hand clasp was and still marks the sealing of a sacred declaration of faith, the symbol of an oath taken when God Mithra and Mithraism as a religion became the creed and confession of a religion new to Rome. At the beginning it was reserved to the military but it was later extended to all classes of people spontaneously or forcibly faithful to the Roman Empire who were eventually admitted to join in the ceremonies that took place in the Mithraea, according to contemporary authors both followers and enemies of Mithraism. Mithraism faded away with the decline of the power and final breakdown of the Empire when Rome became the seat of another new religion later called Christianity that replaced the traditional and official religion of the *urbi et orbi.* (the city [of Rome] and the [Roman] World).

The handclasp of Mithra with the Sun (=Sūrya, Savitṛ), the *dexiosis* or *dexterarum conjunctio* is an agreement, an understanding, a sacred unbreakable alliance, a sacrosanct pact, an oath and promise of correct behaviour, life, love, dedication to a cause, friendship, fair-mindedness, justice and freedom, but it is not a "fusion" of two principles, Mithra and Savitṛ in a single one. The handclasp is the integration of two entities, each retaining its own identity. One, Mithra is the physical, rational though limited human being conscious of having a conscience, the other, Savitṛ is the spiritual, eternal, splendorous and mighty Idea or Being, beyond human comprehension. Physically the *dexiosis* is quite different from the "handshake" of the Romans who grasped each other's right forearm but not the hands, in a firm hold. The Roman "handshake" was meant to declare openly that neither contestant was armed, a promise of fair behaviour and correct intentions before or after the ensuing fight. The handclasp, as represented in the Mithraea, is an emblem that befits well a "military god" as described by Jung, because it represents the loyalty due to the military commanders and ultimately to the Emperor of the Empire.

Modern authors have variously interpreted the meaning of Mithra's handclasp with the Sun and of the inscriptions most commonly engraved or painted on the walls or over the altar of the Mithraea but ultimately they all tend to glorify the attributes and power of Lord Mithra and the obedience due to the Emperor as the personification of Rome and the Roman Empire.

Throughout the Vedas, the *Avesta* and Mithraism, God Mitra/ Mithra remains essentially the same, perfect, unobtrusive and ideal friend as the Āditya Mitra of the earliest hymns of the *Ṛgveda.*

Evolution of the Personality of Varuṇa/Ahura-Mazda

Yasht Khvarshed (=Hvarshed) no. 6 of the Khordah *Avesta* is dedicated to Ahura-Mazda splendid as the Sun, one of Ahura-Mazda's infinite facets. In Vedism, Sūrya is the Sun honoured as a celestial body whom man greets and eulogizes at sunrise and in the evening at sunset. Savitṛ is the name that identifies symbolically the Sun-God, its "spiritual essence". Savitṛ in the Gāyatrī *mantra* of the *Ṛgveda* is eulogised, praised and invoked with the same understanding as Khvarshed (brilliance, greatness, transcendence, light, glory, splendour) throughout the *Avesta* where Ahura-Mazda himself is eulogised and praised as The Only Supreme Entity. Everywhere Mitra/Mithra is celebrated as the Lord of wide pastures, where the word *pastures* holds its symbolic meaning of food for body and spirit of man and kine. The intention, meaning and representations are the same in the *Ṛgveda*'s dual Mitra-Varuṇau as in the *Avesta* and in Mithraism where Mithra (Mitra) is associated but is not the same and not fused with Ahura (Varuṇa)-Mazda (magnificent). Quoting from the *Avesta*:

Yasht Khvarshed, Niyayes no. 6, is dedicated to the Sun.

0. In the name of Ahura-Mazda, visualised as the Sun
1. Homage to you, O Ahura-Mazda, earlier than all Creation. Homage to you Amesa Spenta . . .
5. Homage to Mithra of the vast pastures, eternal, celestial who pervades the Universe to its distant limits
6. We offer this sacrifice to the immortal, radiant Sun who has fast running horses
7. We offer this sacrifice to Mithra Lord of all Space, created by Ahura-Mazda the most glorious of all the spiritual Yazata. May both Mithra and Ahura the most excellent

> come to our help. We offer this sacrifice to the immortal radiant Sun with his swift horses, ready and quick to shine with Splendour. . . .
>
> — A. Alberti, 2008, Yasht Khvarshed; Niyayes

A large number of eloquent quotes could be given here, they are not only literarily beautiful but most meaningful, they are rich with profound, inspired religiosity and spiritual conviction. In Vedism Sūrya is the Sun and Savitṛ who, in the Gāyatrī *mantra* (*Ṛgveda* III.62) is praised and eulogised with the same understanding as the Khvarshed of the *Avesta* (might, brilliance, greatness, transcendence, light, glory, splendour) and is eulogised as a spiritual entity. The intention, meaning and representation are the same in the *Ṛgveda* as in the *Avesta*: the physical heavenly body is the Sun, its value, meaning and "essence" are expressed respectively as "Savitṛ" in the *Ṛgveda* and as Khvarshed in the *Avesta*: glorious and exact behaviour. Both Savitṛ and Khvarshed are the image of Order, Perfect Goodness and Ideal Perfection. God Mithra of Mithraism is the image of the Supreme Being imbued with all optimal qualities, fused in one ideal concept: Mazdeism as a religion.

During its long history and evolution Mitra/Mithra of the Vedas and of the *Avesta* represents but is not embodied or fused with the physical heavenly body known as the Sun. However, the "essence", the "spiritual valence" of the Sun is everywhere and always represented by Savitṛ in the Vedas and by Ahura-Mazda in the *Avesta*. Yasht Khvarshed, no. 6 is entirely dedicated to Ahura-Mazda the Supreme Being. In Mithraism this ideal is symbolised and reminded by the *dexiosis* or *dexterarum conjunctio.* The cult of Mitra/Mithra entered in Rome in the last century BCE and spread over all the lands where the Roman legions marched because of its pragmatism and its willing blind obedience to The Law of the Roman Empire. It survived for centuries in Britannia as the proverbial practicality of the "English people." The same but hypertrophied tendency to pragmatism, expansionism and despotism entered in the Church of Rome and in later time empires and *would-be empires* the world over.

Knowledge of the *Avesta* was widespread in Central Asia, and the ancient kings of northern ancient Iran were known as *kavi*. Originally the term *kavi* meant a "singer, poet, also Prince or King". Entire genealogies of kings bear the honorific title *Kavi* before their name. Noteworthy among them is Kavi Vistaspa reputed powerful patron of Zarathustra. Kavi Vistaspa appears also in the Indian Purāṇic genealogies as a distinguished member of the very important lineage of the Atharvan. The Atharvan and the Aṅgīras were two of the original lineages of Central Asian I-A. They were brāhmaṇa families who were knowledgeable of Agni (fire) and all positive and negative forms and aspects of Fire and warmth, its meaning and attributes, its importance in the dynamics of nature, its role in the collective and individual life and health of mankind and in the appropriate technicalities for the use of fire (Vannucci, 1999). The I-I and I-A worshipped the same ancestral gods and Zarathustra himself preached that the Vedic-Avestic gods Mitra/Mithra and Varuṇa/Ahura are the two immortal benefactors of mankind, they stand at orders of Ahura-Mazda, the only Supreme God. There are many cultural links and personalities common to the *Avesta*, the Vedas, the Brāhmaṇas, the Purāṇas and other sacred texts. Over and above linguistic affinities, they are meaningful and indelible proofs of the common roots of the two ancient I-E people, the I-A and the I-I who first entered in Central Asia at different times as groups of nomads, clans or tribes coming from the Euro-Asian steppes north of the Caspian and Black seas (Ghirshman, map 1977, Vannucci, 2007, etc.) during an undefined number of millennia BCE and later.

Unfortunately an estimated two-third of the entire *Avesta* is lost forever but the oral and written tradition that survived are fair enough to offer a representative idea of the culture and spirituality of the ancient I-I. We know also from the Indian tradition that Aditi, the Infinite, mother of Infinity engendered five sons, Varuṇa, Mitra, Bhaga and the two Aśvins (Twins). To the five original Ādityas other deities were added with the development of these cultures, most important among them in the context of this essay, are Indra and Aryamān. About the Aśvins, also called Nāsatyas, Griffith (1889) writes: "The Aśvins seem to have been a puzzle even to the oldest Indian commentators." Yāska thus refers to them in the *Nirukta* (XII.1): "Next in the order are the deities whose sphere is the heaven; of these the Aśvins are the first to arrive. . . . Who then are these Aśvins? — "Heaven and Earth," say some. . . . They are the earliest bringers of light in the morning sky, who in their chariot hasten onward before the dawn and prepare the sky for her [Uṣā, the Dawn]. . . ." Some hymns of the *R̥gveda* mention Indra's twin (*see R̥V* I.33.14, etc.), named Kutsa, who could have been, as seen from internal evidence a *r̥ṣi* or the founder of a special school. Personally I tend to favour the ancient mental image of the personality of the Aśvins who are frequently present throughout the Vedas, as the *ego* and *alter ego,* or in Jung's terms, the *I* and the *Selbst,* the *pair of opposites* and the internal contradictions and decisions that all thinking beings must face daily throughout their individual lifetime. Invariably the Aśvins are also described as driving each his chariot and being precursors of dawn and sunset respectively. We can extend the concept to the role of the twins, or the "*pair of opposites*" to Ahriman, the ruler of darkness who is said to precede sunrise at dawn "and prepare living beings for the night rest" at sunset.

About the Aśvins, Chakravarty (1997) manifests the same concern,

> *Belief in the divine twins is a universal phenomenon of mythology. Their counterparts in different mythologies have been worshipped by peoples all over the world since very early days of human history. The solar character of them is almost universal. The characteristics of this archetype belonging to the Indo-European tradition are more specifically defined. To mention a few: their association with horse*

and boat, their magical healing power and solar identity, and their also being warriors, saviours at sea and associated to a solar maiden.

To this we could add the constellation of the Twins, almost universally described and named. Pairs of opposites or "pairs of extremes," an ill-defined idea that has been with Man throughout his variegated history and is studied down to present under multiple, physiological, philosophical, psychological and psychiatric aspects. In the present context, pairs of opposites or "pairs of extremes" may be seen as a basic principle of a mentally sane human being. From a pessimistic view, "pairs of extremes" drag men as puppets moving passively or pushed from one to the other member of pairs, such as Good or Bad, Peace or War. From an optimistic viewpoint man's mind can be seen swinging from one to the other extreme eternally trying to find and occasionally actually finding the middle point, the prescribed "middle path" recommended by prince Siddhārtha of the Sākya lineage, later called Gautama the Buddha (563–483), a contemporary of Zarathustra who was born and preached in the sixth century BCE in Chorasmia (=Khwarizm).

The ancient pre-Zarathustra I-I tradition tells us that originally there were two Great Gods who were twins, they were Ormazd or Ohrmazd (Light, perfect Good) and Ahriman (Darkness, total absence of Goodness = *ara* = *angra mainyu*) who is his opposite and opponent. Mazda or Mazdah is the "One who creates with his mind," the mind that sees or perceives everything. Ahura selects as his 20th name: Mazda (Yt. 1, 8) the omniscient (Alberti, 2004). It is not clear at what time the dual Ahura-Mazda was established as a self-existent Power or Spirit. The significant point here is that Mazda or Mazdah is one of the ancient-most gods of the I-I and that the name Ahura, former Varuṇa, was attached to that of Mazda at a late stage of the evolution of Avestism, most probably by Zarathustra himself when it was recognised that the two Supreme entities, Mazda and Varuṇa are essentially one and the same. Among the Indo-

Aryan the meaning of the word Ahura (Asura) is that of a powerful Being gifted with *māyā* (magic power). The name Ahura corresponds to the I-A name Asura that is the name of a very powerful but bad being gifted with great magical power.

The identity of the Ahura/Varuṇa personality of the pre-Zarathustra *Avesta* was discussed above. The point to be made here is that Varuṇa remains the same God in the Vedas as in the Old *Avesta*, namely the unfettered son of Aditi. Among the Indo-Aryan Varuṇa with time is associated to waters in general and is a very close partner of the Sun as Sūrya/Savitṛ (Goodness, Brilliance, Might, Purity) and with Mitra (Order, Law, Justice). Among both Indo-Iranian and Indo-Aryan Sun and Waters are the great benefactors as well as friends of man, because without their existence and joint action there would be no life on Earth. This is the "pair of opposites" or the "action and reaction" or the "exchange of matter and energy" probably represented by the Twins that continuously sustain Life, World and Universe.

The image of Varuṇa as visualised in Brāhmanism, as discussed in the *Śatapatha Brāhmaṇa*, in the *Maitrāyaṇīya Upaniṣad* and throughout the most ancient sacred texts is one of perfect Accuracy, Reality, Fidelity, Justice and unfailing Truth. This is the same image as of Ahura-Mazda that was later incorporated in Mithraism. Water is the materialisation, if I may say so, of the idea of Varuṇa that evolved from Vedism/Avestism, through Mazdeism and Zoroastrianism to Mithraism and beyond. "Varuṇa of the thousand waters, of running waters is Life, he is the Saviour of existence, truth, reality and faith . . . everything that exists takes rest, even the wind may take rest but waters never rest (*Śat*. III.9.2.5) and (*Maitr*., IV.5.4) . . . Waters provide peace and serenity." This symbolism lived and was carried over also materially, in the Mithraea where running water and fresh water pots were always at hand. This Truth is shared in some or other way by all religions and faiths and Varuṇa is everywhere revered under its many forms and myriad names.

As mentioned above I see the Aśvins or "twins" as the figure that describes or defines "the pair of opposites" that are present in nature as the material and immaterial forces on which man has no power. They are well known to psychologists as potential trouble-maker fixed ideas or as manias in the mind of many persons. In normal behaviour the pairs of opposites balance each other to ensure reasonable response to situations or disturbances that would upset the equilibrium of the normal processes of living. The pair of opposites may be the cause of mental or health situations where one pair of the couple becomes reasonably or obstinately opposed to the other member of the pair. The hesitation between the two is normally solved by the person's instinctive, physiological or reasoned response to the situation. However, if no balanced decision is arrived at, serious mental and/or physical disorders may happen. The Aśvins are said to be the precursors who pave the way for Dawn herself to arrive in full glory, an example of a mechanism where natural meteorological phenomena are controlled by the two diligent and well-prepared twins. This is also a mechanism that at other levels may help the human mind out of turmoil and uncertainty. I believe that every normal human being can recognise this from his or her experience. The Aśvins are well prepared to control and normalise abnormal episodic events in Nature or in the inner self of human beings.

Zarathustra lived in the sixth century BCE, when parts of Central Asia were not yet organised as self-contained independent nations. Zarathustra was born and preached in the border area between Chorasmia (Khwarizm) and Sogdiana and his birthplace is stated to be either one or the other. There was well-developed, irrigated agriculture in the region between rivers Amu Daryā and Syr Daryā where he lived, as well as in nearby Bactria and Margiana. Irrigation covered vast areas, transport by land or river was developed though it had gone through troubled periods of lack of maintenance and manpower works due to international politics, wars and invasions by enemies or by climatic changes. The region had attained a high level of culture and technical development as well as regular trade with other people at all levels.

This vast geographic region was inhabited by I-A and I-I people. The *Avesta*, the Vedas and other Indian and other texts, scripts and languages bear evidence to a productive exchange of religious, cultural and technical know-how among all the *Arya*s and between these and other people, up to and throughout the Sassanid Period. Avestism/Mazdeism spread from this part of Central Asia that corresponds to what was then called *Airyānam Vaejo* by the I-I in the *Avesta*. Some of the tribes of the Śakas who roamed in this same region also adopted Mazdeism.

The excavations at Surkh-Kotal and Begram (ancient Kapisa, near present-day Kabul) and at Dura-Europos on the higher Euphrates in ancient Parthia, show that Mazdeism was adopted early even as other religions survived in the extensive area from Parthia eastwards beyond the river Syr Daryā. Under the Sassanids (*c.* CE 226 to 651) Mazdeism or Zoroastrianism was dominant since the second century BCE, it flourished in northern Iran and continued to be the common religion also in Phars, in the south-west, even after the Sassanids came to power (Dani and Litvinsky, 1996). Zoroastrianism along with Buddhism became the state religion and was also the leading faith among the Śakas who were a branch of the Scythians, and to some degree also of the Pahlavas of India. Kauṭilya (in *Arthaśāstra* 2.36.1-4, *see* Litvinsky, 1996) states that Buddhism was an important factor in urban development and city administration during the Kuṣāṇa period (first century CE to fourth century CE).

From the Achaemenid Period Onwards
Roman Mithraism: Recapitulation

During and after the period of the Achaemenid dynasty and partly under the influence of the Graeco-Roman culture, the

Sun itself becomes an associate (*socius*) of Mithra as the Giver of Life and there was a revival of the semi-forgotten rites due to Āditya Mitra. The *leontocephalus* present in almost all Mithraea is embroiled in the tight coils of a vicious snake that represents the evil forces of the dark, cold, below-ground netherworld from where man may perhaps escape, but only if he accepts and follows the laws of Nature and those of cultured man. Mithra on the other hand is everywhere eulogised, he is undefeated (*invictus*), Lord omnipotent like the Sun and is said to be "SOLI DEO INVICTO MITRAE" (To the undefeated Mitra who is like the Sun; or: To the only Sun-God Undefeated Mitra) *see*: Cumont, *Textes*, also others among the most common invocations, praises and various forms of worship, thanksgiving, prayers and other rituals found engraved or otherwise figured in the very numerous functional Mithraea, up to the fifth/sixth centuries CE. Numerous graffiti, incisions or paintings having about the same meaning and context have survived to this day, though the sites have lost their role as places of worship for the followers of God Mithra.

Mitra as a name or an adjective survives as an archetype inbuilt in the mind and reason of every person; he teaches and helps us to discriminate between good and bad, correct or not, true and false and then he entrusts our conscience with the responsibility of taking a decision or following the earlier or a newly prescribed course of action. Man has the freedom to decide on his actions, he should be grateful forever to Mitra for preparing him to do so.[11, 12]

Though most of the Vedas are still available, only an estimated third of the *Avesta* and *Zend-Avesta* survived historic vandalism. However, what remains offers a reasonably complete understanding of the teachings and wisdom of Zarathustra and of the ancient *magi*, the priestly class of the Medes and Persians. About or more than two-thirds of the entire I-I tradition succumbed to the violence of wars, civil and religious bigotry and a variety of political demeanours. The chronologically oldest hymns mention *airyānam vaejaḥ* as the original homeland of the Aryan (I-I) people, but the *gāthā* of the *Avesta*, as we have it, were not contemporaneous with the collection of *gāthā* of the I-A. The contents of the two texts are not alike and they were probably composed at different time periods though both belong to the ancient-most stage of musical and literary expression of the Central Asian I-E. Based on grammatical and syntactic characteristics of the language used by both, a relative chronology of the *gāthā*s of the two cultures and of the numerous interpolations present in the texts has tentatively been drawn by scholars. The *gāthā*s were found not to correspond to one another chronologically, but to be comparable as cultural level and meaning. Clearly the schism between the two cultures happened at an early stage when only the original basic beliefs of their naturalistic religion had been formulated and when major geographic displacements of the groups or tribes of all the Arya were still underway. Undoubtedly the Indo-Iranian diverged from the Indo-Aryan people before the full development of the rich Ṛgvedic pantheon (Bhargava, loc. cit.).

With cultural evolution over the centuries, the Indo-Aryan Mitra himself becomes differentiated into several gods and deities specialised and appropriate to the complexities of settled life such as organised trade, administration of the land, urbanisation, developed agriculture, engineering, defence and attack warfare, technical developments and metal works, grammatical improvement of the spoken language, and inventions typical of growing social stratification and specialisation, and others. Mitra of fully developed Hinduism is often remembered directly or indirectly; above and beyond his new attributes the god continues to be inevitably invoked in matters related to Order, Law, Duty and above all, Justice. Goddess Demeter (Demetra) of ancient Greece has very much the same characteristics, besides having the merit of having introduced "bread wheat," an improved variety of wheat, in Attica, as early as the middle fifteenth century BCE (Vannucci, 1998), dated by circumstantial evidence, namely the mention of King Pandion and of his queen as patrons of Demeter herself and by palynological data.[12]

Perhaps the teachings of Zarathustra were not the only cause or the first disagreement and enmity between the two cultures and people, none the less the new beliefs and philosophy preached by the Prophet created a strong antagonism between them that grew with time. From the last century of the last millennium BCE onwards, the I-A and the I-I or Persians as the I-I were called already during the Achaemenid period, drifted more and more apart though they all continued to call themselves Arya.

In the *Avesta* Mithra is remembered, invoked, prayed to most often indirectly as "Lord of the ample prairies, Lord of vast lands." Mithra is the Great Judge, the Great Friend of Law, of Order, of Measure and of Mankind where men are considered collectively and individually. Reading over and over again what of the *Avesta* has come down to us from the past, specially the oldest *gāthā*, Mithra may be seen above all as the Lord of Justice, Lord of prescribed rites and rituals invented by man and as the Lord of correct ethical proportions, behaviour and reason. God Mithra is the representative and protector of the people and of the movements of a nomadic society. This injunction was reinforced as the nomads became settled, with growing urbanism and with the practice of regular transhumance that is a corollary of the growth of settled life and urbanism. There is no doubt that it was mostly due to the advent and preaching of the Prophet that many groups and classes of I-I people and other I-E clans who had moved towards Central Asia were united from the social and linguistic points of view, including with the respect of each other's religious beliefs. The most characteristic example of this is the gradual mixing of the Medes with the I-I and

Persians. By the middle of the last millennium BCE nation building was politically achieved under the Achaemenid kings and was later expanded under Sassanid rule. A rock relief of Darius I at Bisutun, here *fig.* 5 (from Dandamayev (1996, in UNESCO, vol. II) shows King Darius (lived 558–486 BCE), double bow in the lowered left hand, with the right hand held up in a gesture of command and attention, the right foot firmly set on a rock about 30 cm high (or a bent-down slave according to other authors) receiving a group of prisoners, hands tied behind their back.

There are many specially noticeable details in this dated relief; *First* — behind the king two royal guards are shown, one holds in the left hand a simple, non compound bow, the second holds with both hands a long Persian lance, the guards follow the Royal Figure and represent his power; *Second* — at the end of the line of prisoners, ". . . a captive is shown . . . taller and with hands tied behind his back, wearing a sharp pointed cap some 30 cm tall . . . probably the chief of the *Saka Tigraxauda* . . . whom . . . Darius replaced by another chief of the same tribe"; *Third* and most important is the large relief of the emblem or symbol of Ahura-Mazda carved immediately above the first four men of the line of captives. Darius campaigned against the tribe of the *Saka Tigraxauda* in 519 BCE, a fixed historical date.

Another representative document is here *fig.* 7 (*apud* Dandamayev, 1996, in UNESCO vol. II) redrawn from the imprint of a cylinder seal showing a hunting scene also of King Darius I. Over the chariot the symbol of Ahura-Mazda is shown very large with long and wide wings fully extended. Several other details such as the role and importance of the date palm, the harness of the two horses and the structural details of the chariot and wheel are eloquent testimonials of the cultural and technical level of the I-I at the time of Darius I and following centuries, as was also described by the classic Greek and Roman authors. The cuneiform script on the side is probably in Aramaic language according to authors.

About 725 years later already in the Sassanid period, Ardashir I proclaimed himself king in year CE 205. At Naqsh-i Rustam a low relief sculpture shows Ardashir, receiving the kingly investiture from Ahura-Mazda himself, here *fig.* 6 (*apud* Litvinsky, 1996, in UNESCO, II). Both the Supreme God and the newly self-proclaimed king are on horseback, they are shown in profile, the two horses standing forehead to forehead. The two human figures represent Ardashir and Ahura-Mazda respectively, both riders are stirrupless, as may be seen by the position of their legs. They grasp the same voluminous ring the size of the head of a human body with a tight grip of their right hand. The ring, a symbol of alliance is shown flat and in full view above the lowered heads of the mounts of the king and of the God. The meaning and value is probably the same as that of the ring figured in the stereotype winged emblem and symbol of the great God Ahura-Mazda where a large ring encircles the body of the God whose wings are shown wide open. In this relief the ring is held on either side by the right hands of the God and of the king. It is the symbol of the power and protection given by the Supreme God Ahura-Mazda to the victorious founder of the Sassanid dynasty. Also the photo of the relief at Naqsh-i Rustam shows badly weathered remains of the relief of the head of Ahura-Mazda carved just above the ring held by the right hands of God and king.

The symbol showing God and king holding together the investiture circular ring is repeated throughout the Sassanid period though it is not always evident in the late period. It is tempting to figure the *dexiosis* of Roman Mithraism as an alternate or derivate form of the same conviction figured in Sassanid Iran where God and Man grasp the single heavy ring, a symbol of alliance between the two powers. The many meanings and symbolism of the circle also come to mind here.

The early stereotype symbol of Mazdeism and of God Ahura-Mazda shown at Bisutun not far from Susa in ancient Media to commemorate the Investiture of Achaemenid king Darius I, here *fig.* 6 (Dandamayev, 1996, in *UNESCO*, vol. II), shows the Supreme God in profile, hands joined at breast height, the body encircled by a numinous ring twice the width of the body and placed flat in full view while the lower half of the body of the Supreme God is hidden by a garment made of 10 pleats. The symbol of Ahura-Mazda is large enough to cover three or five of the first prisoners in the row moving towards King Darius I. Two large wings are fully stretched open at right and left of the figure, they correspond to the front and rear of the God who is seen in profile. From the point of view of this Essay it is important to note that Mazda was already an established god at the time of Zarathustra and before the sovereignty of the Achaemenid dynasty.

Although much of the *Avesta* is a libel against the *daeva* worshippers, meaning the I-A, the Indo-Iranians retained some of the early-most representative gods of the early I-E of Central Asia. The orderly, generous and good, faithful friend and devoted God Mithra, the knower of the Cosmic Law, sits on the *Cinvat* bridge to judge the soul of the deceased since the beginning of time. Mithra is almost as frequently invoked as the *"great beyond-reach"* Ahura-Mazda, the Light, the Splendour, the Mightiest Being that IS, that EXISTS. The *Avesta* includes the *songs* (hymns) of the Indo-Iranians as the Vedas include those of the Indo-Aryans that are known at present. Music, in its melodic and rhythmic forms, is one of the key factors in the processes of acculturation of most civilisations. The *mantras* (*manthras*) collected in the Vedas are under the form of psalms, rhythmic chants and metric poetry. It is easier to memorise, remember and repeat correctly poetry and melodic music, than prose. The successful ancient tradition of memorising the Vedas is alive to date and there are many learned brāhmaṇas who know by heart the *Ṛgveda* and also a second, third and fourth Veda. The ancient musical tradition is still alive in India where music and rhythmic poetry have been a powerful means for the preservation of the *mantra*s of the Vedas that survived practically intact through centuries and disasters. It is also known that much of the ancient I-I hymns and probably also other religious texts that were destroyed in historical times, had been transmitted orally and most probably in rhythmic or other musical forms.[13]

The I-I and other people of Central Asia adopted diverse forms of script, most important among them was the cuneiform in its variant and derived forms. Aramaic was one of the most commonly spoken languages of the masses, at least up to the time of the rise of the Kuṣāṇa. The I-A relied more on the oral tradition and on Sanskrit and derived languages as the regular medium of transmission of intellectual, religious and cultural knowledge in general. Rites and rituals as well as philosophical writings including astronomy and mathematics were initially almost exclusively known and used by the priestly class. Writing of the sacred texts was adopted only as late as the first centuries CE or later. There are no chronological data on the undefinable beginning of the oral tradition. Archaeology, iconography and epigraphy, besides the written and oral traditions, are the most useful and reliable tools for the study of the very ancient culture and of the geographic displacements of all the Arya people who entered early in Central Asia. We find the decided, strong but quiet and unremitting presence of Vedic God Mitra everywhere and ever (see Chapter 7 — Appendix).

The historical Indo-Aryan written tradition started late. Beyond mythology, the Vedas were followed by the Vedānta texts, the Itihāsas, the Purāṇas, the epics and the very rich Indian profane, secular, histrionic and scientific literature on a great variety of subjects that were recorded in various languages and scripts at different times. The oral tradition was memorised as songs, beginning with the original seven *ṛṣis* who were followed by a large class of learned men and women. The Indian oral tradition does not include only religious texts, it includes and classifies also all matters of knowledge, habits, customs, practicalities and technicalities, mythology, astronomy, medicine, religion, history, social sciences, genealogies and family life, all the branches of Natural Sciences and much more, most of which was recorded in writing only late, after long and very long periods when the transfer of knowledge from one generation to the following, from *guru* to *śiṣya*, was mainly through education, example and participation of all, young, adults and elders in all matters concerning the family, the highly structured society and the religious daily life and practices. The oral tradition includes music, singing and dancing, stage performance, story telling and more to be performed under the tutelage of both human and divine patrons. Performers formed groups of specialists or "castes". The same is true for all the crafts and technical arts, most important among them is that of the *lohārī*s or metal workers, of the potters, the singers, the actors, all others. Several arts and crafts are still practised with traditional methods. Most remarkable is the art of making from small to very large bronze statues, famous among them the *Cola* bronzes most often made by the method of the *cire perdue* (lost wax technique) by specialised artisans working under the guidance of learned brāhmaṇas. To date both artisans and brāhmaṇas belong to their respective traditional caste and sub-caste and they all work together.

Differently from the story of the I-A literature, the early oral tradition of the I-I has not come down to us organised methodically as the Vedas and Vedānta literature have come. Fortunately, the Persian historiographer Abdul Kasim Firdausi (CE 940–1020) put in writing much of the early history of the Indo-Iranian people in his famous book, the *Shāhnāmeh*.

We know that most of the early "songs" or hymns and other texts of the *Avesta* are ancient and were created before and after the advent of Zarathustra though some may have been modified following his teachings. The cultural revolution created by

Zarathustra occurred at a time when various scripts were already in use in Asia and the phonetic phoenician/Greek alphabets could be easily adapted to be recorded in writing form and thereby perpetuate the understanding and use of various languages and dialects, including Aramaic and Sanskrit-derived old I-I.

The I-A Indians moved from Central Asia very far South and Eastwards, over deserts and mountains and the strictly Indian culture remained closed upon itself for a long period of time because of its own nature, its social structure, the unavoidable sharing of living space in the Indian subcontinent with people of different cultural backgrounds and finally because of ecologic/geographical constraints. The Zarathustra movement directed Mazdeism, the religion of Ahura-Mazda, into avenues new and different from the original common I-E culture. Though the name of the religion is now known as Zoroastrianism in the West and though the Prophet's name is usually known at present as Zoroaster, it was since the ruling of the Achaemenid dynasty in Persia (Phars, southern Iran) and from the last centuries BCE onwards that Mithraism, an offshoot of Mazdeism established itself as a well-structured religion, including habits, cultic practices, philosophy, liturgy, texts and everyday way of life.

The earliest undated records that have come down to us are to be read in the *Ṛgveda* where we see Mitra closely associated to Varuṇa, the only unfettered son of Aditi. The two Ādityas complement each other, together they uphold The Law and they rule over Earth and Sky. They are guardians of cultic practices, rites and rituals, they punish sin, untruth and wicked behaviour and as such they entered in Rome with the Mithraea.

Coming back to the subject of iconography I wish to recall here that the fourth degree of the initiation of the postulants to the mysteries of God Mitra, the god of the religion new to Roma, was the Lion (*leo*) that had planet Jupiter as its symbol. The emblem of this degree was the *leontocephalus,* a large frightening figure of a human body with a lion head.

The name *leontocephalus* (*lion-headed[man*] in Latin) is a literal translation from Sanskrit *narasiṁha =man-lion;* also in the *Īśa Upaniṣad,* a name given to a fantastic creature depicted as a winged man with a lion head carrying keys and a torch in his hands while his body is embroiled in the coils of a wicked serpent. The latter detail may perhaps best be understood as a representation of the punishment inflicted by Varuṇa (Ahura) on wicked persons. Al-Biruni makes a detailed study of the Indian myth of *narasiṁha* whose appearance in the morning and disappearance in the evening mark the moment of the *saṁdhi* in the Indian astronomical system (*see* also Chapter 7, Appendix). The figure of the *leontocephalus* has been described and interpreted by modern authors in a variety of manners though the "man-lion" of Mithraism can be readily identified as *narasiṁha,* the fourth *avatāra* of Viṣṇu who was created to protect child Prahlāda from his wicked father Hiraṇyakaśipu.

Besides historical data, the present study also draws basic information from Vedic figures and Purāṇic myths, their meaning and scientific significance, many of them meticulously analysed by al-Biruni. Some of these are particularly pertinent in the context of this short essay. One such is the tale of child Dhruva, son of king Uttānapāda, immortalised as the Pole Star for his fixed unshakable devotion to Lord Viṣṇu. Dhruva is the personification of *permanence,* he is fixed, he has unshakable determination and sense of duty. Equally meaningful is the devotion of child Prahlāda who could see the Lord everywhere and in everything and who could sense the relative weight and measurability of non-material mathematical quantities. Prahlāda's wicked father, the *daiva* king Hiraṇyakaśipu enquired whether God was present everywhere and when child Prahlāda replied that He was present also in the stone column in front of him, the king hit it with a stick and from the pillar emerged the frightful lion-headed monster. This tale is here shortened from the Purāṇas and Upaniṣads (*see* also the *Puranas*, by Mazumdar, 2005). Ossanna (1988) discusses some of the many different interpretations of the symbolism and meaning of the *leontocephalus* and comes to the conclusion "that it is not easy to conclude what exactly is the meaning of the monstrous and mysterious *leontocephalus* . . . evidently linked to the Mitra cult." The figure in Ossanna shows the creature emerging or leaning on a large rock.

The *leontocephalus* is depicted in most Mithraea of the Roman period, but what to my knowledge has not been pointed out is that the Roman word *leontocephalus* is exactly the Latin translation of the Sanskrit word *narasiṁha* (man-lion), namely the fourth incarnation of Viṣṇu, the *avatāra* that is the symbol of the development of *consciousness* that reaches the highest level in Man (*see* Anonymous, Sanskrit Glossary). Radhakrishnan (*The Principal Upanishads*, I published 1953, fourth impression 1974) says in the introduction to the *Īśa Upaniṣad* that belongs to the Vājasaneyī school of the *Yajurveda*

> *Its main purpose is to teach the essential unity of God and the world, being and becoming. It is interested not so much in the Absolute itself, Parabrahman, as in the Absolute in relation to the world, Parameśvara. It teaches that life in the world and life in the Divine Spirit are not incompatible.*

I believe that the identity of the *leontocephalus* with *narasiṁha* cannot be doubted, both characters have the same value and meaning.

The first three incarnations of Viṣṇu are *matsya* (fish); *kūrma* (tortoise) and *varāha* (boar). The three taken together and in this order, recall the figure of *Mitra petragenus* (*petra genetrix* = produced by the rock, the good earth, the evolution of the forms of life). The fourth incarnation of Viṣṇu, as mentioned above, is *narasiṁha*, the man-lion that represents, both in the Mithraea of the Roman world as in the first steps of the ritual for the initiation of the neophytes to the religion of God Mithra, the *leontocephalus* represents, similarly to *narasiṁha*, the *avatāra* of Viṣṇu, the emergence of conscience in Man. To be conscious of having a conscience is what makes man a Man (*see* Jung), different from other animals.[14]

Al-Biruni (973-1048) was born in what is now Uzbekistan, in the ancient city of Kaṭh in what was then called Chorasmia (Khwarizm). For this reason al-Biruni is frequently called "the Khwarizmian" astronomer, mathematician and philosopher. Al-Biruni refers frequently to ancient India's science and to the oral tradition and myths, much of it preserved in the Purāṇic texts, to discuss their objective validity, showing once more that correct science can be offered as an easy reading for the general public to absorb philosophical truths. In the present context what is meaningful is the survival of ancient Vedic *mantras* and myths intact with their original meaning along with their adoption by the contemporary garb of Roman temples to Mitra.[15]

Mitra and Varuṇa reward goodness, correct behaviour and obeisance to the law (*see* *ṚV* I; II.89). They are mighty and powerful, hence they are also addressed as "kings" who uphold the Law and Order of the Universe, personified as the Universal Mother Aditi. They give protection to man "with all aids" and they make him rich. In a late hymn Mitra is invoked as the God who stimulates men to work, who sustains earth and sky, prepares the oil for the oblations, frees man from sickness, wounds and fear, and is the God who *sustains the sacred Law.* Like the *Avestan Mithra* the *Ṛgvedic Mitra* also sustains all gods and their worshippers (*Ṛgveda* III.59.9). Since he is "measure" and "proportion" personified, Mitra regulates everything and is continuously present in the life of all living and non-living beings, and also after death of the body. Mitr, Mitra, Mithra, Mythra are one and the same God, though the name is variously spelled along time and space.

The theology and theogony of the Vedas or of the *Avesta* are not explained in the ancient texts of India and Iran in the present sense of the verb "to explain," but many of the essential thoughts and arguments of the ethical world of the Vedas, and even more of Vedānta, were assimilated and elaborated upon by Mithraism, though on a divergent path from Vedism. There is a direct line of thought from the ancient common root of the I-A and I-I people that is most clearly represented by the Mitra (Mithra) present in the Universe and begotten by Aditi. Mithraism, a religion heir to the ancient Veda and Vedānta ideology and philosophy is not an unwanted burden placed on man's shoulders and mind, it is instead a protecting and helpful guardian and a mental system symbolised by the *handclasp* that entered in Rome with Mythraism. Mitra's handclasp with the Sun God must not be confused or translated as the handshake of the Romans that has a different story and meaning behind it and is also physically a different sort of grasp.

In a short story taken from real life Vannucci (2004) recalls a scene when she lived for some time in the high ranges of Garhwal in the Western Himalaya. A sitting *pahāṛī* (man from the mountains) was stroking and chanting softly to a dying horse whose head was cradled in his lap while another *pahāṛī* applied soothing balms on the open fracture of the horse's leg. Both men were intensely centred in their mental, spiritual action intended to ease the suffering of "our friend, *HAMĀRĀ MITRA* who has worked with us for so many years": fidelity, faithfulness, love and loving care must be vouchsafed unto a beloved friend and partner in life, specially on the occasion of the passage unto another existence — in the name and loving care of Mitra. It is an ethical duty of every human being towards any other living being.

La stretta di mano. Il contenuto etico della Religione di Mitra (The handclasp, the ethical content of the religion of Mitra) by Ossanna (1988)[16] is one of the recent books in the already long series of translations, studies and analyses of Mazdeism, of God Mithra and of Mithraism. Ossanna produced an exhaustive bibliography and clears many of the hitherto debated or wrong ideas about Mithraism. Mithraism or Mithraic Faith is the religion of God Mithra that took shape after this God entered and was established in Rome and throughout the Roman Empire. Mithraism is a protecting and helpful guardian and mental system symbolised by the *handclasp*.

Ossanna's text is inspired with understanding of the profound meaning of Mithra's personality, value and teachings. The author begins the Introduction with the words (tr. mine):

> *I first heard the name of Mitra when I was a child in a [rural] elementary school. In a field near the school [in the Non Valley of the Trentino region of the Italian Alps] a peasant had unearthed a sculpted stone engraved with the image of a deity worshipped many centuries earlier by our ancestors. The teacher . . . told us about the very ancient religion and of the youth* [*shown on the carving*] *who killed a bull to fertilise the land with its blood. That young man, friend of the Sun — the great God of light and warmth — with his generous feat had provided herbs for animals, wheat for man and security to all men for the joy of living.*

Ossanna further states that *"this work of mine* [the book] *is about the ethical content of "Mithraism" because so much has otherwise already been written about Mitra."*

The *Avesta* (at several places, specially in the *Videvdad*) mentions the places where sacrifices to Mithra were held and describes the wood made ready for the fire, the meat and milk for the offering and the mortar and pestle used to press the *haoma* (*soma*) plant to obtain its juice, however these are not to be seen in the representations, figures and photos taken from the Mithraea that are known at present. Due to logistic, spatial, oral and early literal tradition it appears doubtful that killing of the bull and perhaps other bloody sacrifices were carried out in the inner space of the Mithraea during the CE period, though they were the rule among the very ancient I-I and I-A. Christian authors of the first centuries CE mention the bloody rituals of the *pagans*: "among them there are also followers of the *pagan* god Mitra" (Tertullian and other early Christian authors). However many of these stories appear to be tendentious.

A few words about the iconography that best helps to interpret Mithraism at its beginning in the Roman period. In most Mithraea there is a sequence of usually eight paintings, mosaics, sculptures or other figures. The first five represent the hieratic degrees of the initiation of the neophytes or postulants to the religion new to them with the symbol of the protective deities at each step. The crow is the symbol of the first degree (*see* Ossanna), it recalls Mithra who brings the fruits of the land. In the second degree Mithra holds bow and arrows, he aims at the rock from where legendary infant Mithra emerged and from which water springs forth for the sake of mankind and all living beings. The third shows Mithra collecting leaves to cover his nudity and fruits to satiate his appetite. The fourth shows Mithra facing the Sun God, the two deities hold hands in a secure hold (in Italian: *la stretta di mano* = the handclasp, *dexiosis* or *dexterarum conjunctio* in Latin). Usually the fourth is the last figure of the series that summarises the mythical story of the Roman God Mithra, including his association with the Sun and his own *solarisation*. This series is not represented exactly in this manner in all Mithraea, however the three or four initial figures of the series of seven or eight are everywhere comparable because they represent the obligatory first four steps of the initiation of the postulants to this doctrine. Quoting from Ossanna (loc. cit.), scholars agree that the gesture of Mithra and his handclasp with the Sun God is an act of *love for mankind* and not a cultic act addressed to God, for this reason Mithra (Mitra) is thanked also by the Sun God.

A 5th image may be present and when so, it is the sacrifice of the very young bull that could be interpreted as the origin of life on Earth that followed the killing of the bull and the fertilisation of the good soil of Mother Earth, where the bull would be the *scapegoat* of Mithraism. The size of the two figures, the beardless youngster with the Phrygian cap and the young bull often shown still hornless and controlled by the very young man, suggest that the image represents the belief in a primordial act and fact of man's own place in nature. The two figures, bullock and man are small and definitely represent two very young promising creatures. The ancient rite eventually was remembered and perhaps worshipped as a symbol, though it no longer had or would be repeated materially or ritualistically.

Other three figures may be present in the series making a total of eight, usually placed four, one above the other on either side of the central figure over the altar. The most frequently present large image over the altar illustrates the *tauroctony,* the killing (?) or blood-letting of the bull. The eight images recall the steps of the initiation rite, they were often arranged into a mosaic on the path leading to the temple, or any other place. Reliefs and sculptures in the round, paintings and inscriptions are present in all the temples to Roman Mithra for the education of the devotees and/or initiation of the neophytes. An interesting sentence in Tertullian's *Apologeticum,* dated CE 197 (Introduction by Moreschini, 2008, ed. BUR, tr. L. Russo) mentions that "the Persians represent the Sun [Mithra] *'painted'* [*sic*] on linen cloth *linteo depictum*)." References to religious paintings on cloth, either linen or cotton are rare, most similar paintings could have been lost over the centuries because of natural material decay.

Mithraism as a reborn religion under Rome adjusted itself to a variety of environments and to cultures different from the original ancestral culture. Mithraea are found from the Iberian peninsula in the West to ancient Persepolis in the East, from Scotland in the North to North Africa and Oxyrhynchos in the Nile Valley in the South. An interesting point about the representation of the *tauroctony* (killing of the bull) is that the bull is controlled by young man Mithra holding the animal's head backwards over its shoulders and is mostly, but not everywhere shown with two fingers of the left hand placed in the nostrils of the animal. I would recall that this was the traditional manner used by the Śakas (a branch of the Scyths) to kill the bull offered in sacrifice to their gods: a man would ride on the bull's neck, would thrust his fingers in the animal's nostrils and then bringing the head backwards with a jerk he would break the vertebral column of the bull's neck. The man could then thrust a dagger in the jugular vein of the animal, exactly as shown in most representations of the *tauroctony* ritual.

As a historical marker I quote Harmatta who mentions that Darius I in his war against the Scyths reached the Aral Sea at the mouth of the river Araxsha [Araxes for Herodotus] which is modern "Amu Daryā", in the year 519 BCE, a valuable exact historical date important in the context of the present essay. Traditional rituals and new rites imported from a variety of cultures and geographic origins are closely matched by the iconography present in the Mithraea where persons of every social order, varying with the place where the temple stood, were admitted to participate or just witness the rites. At some places and time over the vast domain even non-initiated persons could participate in the rites and rituals.

Again quoting from Ossanna *ipsis litteris*: "Going beyond the historical and mythical reality, there is no doubt that Mithra, friend, faithful ally and companion, guarantor of faithfulness and himself an image of Life, there is no doubt that Mithra serves an ethical function" bearing in mind that "the Law is the same for every human being." I would further stress that the rules and laws of Mithraism correspond exactly to the image and role of God Mitra in Vedism and in Avestism. Also in the *Avesta* Mithra is represented as the personification of Law, Justice, Loyalty, Friendship, Honesty, Faithfulness and all of these and more are fortified and sanctified by the handclasp, the *dexterarum conjunctio*. There is no need to search for the origin of the Avestan and Persian Mithra in ancient cultures and gods other than the Vedic Mitra (Mithra). Vedic Mitra passes directly from one archaic cultural tradition to its twin tradition, from Vedism to Avestism then to Zoroastrianism/Mazdeism in the latest stages of the long story of Āditya Mitra, begotten son of Aditi. As Dandekar said (1997) "everything evolves with time, even gods evolve." Also common to the *Ṛgveda* and the *Avesta* is the respectful behaviour of avoiding calling the god or any "higher up" by name instead of using his or her title. It is just a question of good manners that is still in use in Asia and some Western cultures, including Europe until recent times. Even at present in Italy respect commands to address a "superior" or "elder" by his title and not by name. In the *Avesta* Mithra is usually addressed to indirectly, as the *yazata* who presides on the preparation and implementation of treaties, contracts and pacts. Mithra is the Great Sovereign Judge who sits on the *Cinvat* bridge to judge the souls of the deceased. The name Mithra, however, is only very rarely fully spelled out in the texts, he is usually recalled naming his attributes, hence the error of some contemporary authors who mistakenly say that Mitra is not an important god since he is only very seldom mentioned in the Vedas.

The Lord Mithra of the *Avesta* is more often mentioned indirectly, he is evoked as a *reminder* to the faithful of the ideals of Mazdeism, frequently repeated throughout the sacred book and expressed as: "good thoughts, good words, good actions." Zarathustra prays to, invokes or addresses the Supreme Spirit Ahura-Mazda directly and in the third person. Mazdeism does not oblige each one of us to be perfect, every human being is in fact *free*. This is the fundamental difference between Man and animals and though not spelt as such, I would say that Mazdeism or Mithraism teaches that man should always listen to the consciousness that Ahura-Mazda has placed in each one of us, if we would only take the trouble to listen to it. The freedom of human beings is not only recognised and admitted, it is *recommended*. Man has the freedom to act according to his own will and should remember that he can be loved by God provided his behaviour is within the ethics preached by Zarathustra who speaks in the name of Ahura-Mazda. Mazdeism as a religion is a "way of life," not an imposition, it does not oblige everyone of us to be perfect. It is an advice and a recommendation of a correct behaviour for the sake of "peace of mind and joy of living." There is a constant reminder that Evil in any of its many forms should be avoided, and one of the many good reasons for this is that the soul of all the deceased will have to cross the *Cinvat* bridge where it will be judged by Mithra before being admitted to the netherworld. If I may say so, Mithra teaches man to be conscious of having a conscience and man should think, speak and act accordingly. Man should always bear in mind that he, and only himself is responsible for his acts.

As mentioned above, perhaps the first *historically dated and documented* presence of Mitra as the God of Law and Justice was when he was called to survey the writing and then to certify the sealing of the famous Treaty that concluded the peace between the Hittites and the Egyptians following the Battle of Qadesh, *c.* 1275 BCE. It had taken many years to finalise the text of the Treaty which had been prepared by the Hittite chancellery after the inconclusive battle waged between them and the Egyptians guided by the young pharaoh Ramses II, about 700 years *before* the birth of Zarathustra. The gods of the Hittites present at the ceremony for "placing the seals" on the document were the traditional ancient I-A gods, prominent among them was Mitra, the preserver and guardian of Pacts and Laws (Vannucci, 2007 and forthcoming). The Lord of Tempests, the most powerful of the Hurrian people's God was also present at the signing of the Treaty because the Hurrian people were the majority of the population of the Hittite kingdom though the rulers were mostly I-A or had Aryanised names. Earlier presence of Ṛgvedic Gods is regularly recorded also in other documents of the Annals of the Hittite Chancellery.

Beyond Mother Earth represented by the rocks from where emerges infant Mithra, there are other archetypes that survive in the iconography of Mithraism. In the late images of the *tauroctony* the snake, the scorpion and the dog are also almost invariably present. The dog and the snake are shown licking the blood that oozes out of the cut made by young Mitra's dagger in the jugular vein of the bull. The brave young man riding the bull has his head turned backwards, a move suggesting that the youth looks for and finds a sign of approval by some "higher up" who overlooks from behind. This is the Sun who in some of the images is readily recognisable as the rays that shine on the successful young man or is represented as a crown of rays at the back of his head. In fact, Mitra searches for approval from his *mitr,* his *alter ego,* the Sun. In most Mithraea there are specially oriented openings in the ceiling that direct the rays of the rising Sun on the figure of the valiant Mithra who presides on the altar.

Some questions could be raised at this point. Is the young man on the back of the young bull with his eyes turned to search approval from higher powers, is that one the same as the traditional ancient Mitra of Vedic memory? Would there have been new myths introduced from other cultures or a complement and variants of the old myth, saying that the killing of the bull was not done by Mitra the Elder himself, but by a new younger Mithra? Would the Phrygian cap used by the younger Mithra be a sign that due to the passage of time and territorial displacements the bull is not killed by the ancient Mithra but by a later incarnation? Would there have been some other myth that has not reached down to us saying that the killing of the bull was not done personally by Mithra but by another and new Power, perhaps the personalised young Roman Empire? Was perhaps this youngster the divinisation of the Emperor, a move recommended by the ego of Julius Caesar? Would the Phrygian cap used by Mithra be the sign that in the geographic expansion of the god, the Phrygians played an important political role for accepting Mithraism as a new or additional Faith worth of the Empire? Mithra is portrayed as a beardless youngster, the bullock is likewise very young and still hornless in many presentations. Is Mithraism a re-interpretation or a new development of Mazdeism? Is the *tauroctony* a return to ancient myths, or just a new ritual of the liturgy developed in Rome and/or by Romans? There have been almost as many interpretations of the *tauroctony* as authors who have expressed their opinion on the matter. What is certain is that such an important and bloody ritual is not within the strict spirit of the original Mazdeism, though it existed in ancient Vedism and Avestism. Would the *tauroctony* suggest a divergence of Mithraism from the ancient tradition or alternately could it be a return to it? Would it be an adaptation to imperial Rome's addiction to violence: *"panem et circenses"* (*bread and circus games* [to be offered to the plebe]) or would it be just the expression of a military god best suited to the imperialism of Rome? Was the *tauroctony* still practised after Mithraism was introduced in Rome or was it retained only as an atavistic symbol? Incidentally I would notice that the *tauroctony* has nothing in common with the myth and ritual killing of Mahiṣāsura in Hindu mythology. Mahiṣāsura had been turned into a buffalo and had to be killed to put the universe back in order. Durgā was the killer of the demon and some tribes and people from remote places, specially in the mountains, such as the *Gurkha* still impersonate the ritual to express their gratefulness to goddess Durgā for the killing of that particularly evil buffalo. The killing of the buffalo by a single violent cut with a sword is therefore related to an entirely different myth.

Few more words about iconography. Much has been written about the symbolism of the snake (serpent) in relation to Mithra and otherwise. There is nothing to be added here. The snake is an archetype present in most cultures and in the instinctive negative reaction against snakes, dragons, serpents and all underground sub-reptitious animals, a disgust that all humans have since childhood. God Mitra, begotten by Aditi was like all the other Ādityas and all human beings except Varuṇa (Ahura) was bound by "fetters" that represent limitations imposed on every living being. These limitations in present terms must be understood as ethical, ethnological and ecological restraints and constraints. The snake lives in the soil, a representation of hidden, devious and dubious thoughts and actions, a fiend and dangerous advisor, producer of venom. Mithraism was introduced in Rome at a time of crises, civil wars, decline of ancestral habits and virtues, of honesty and pride, and of cupidity growing beyond the capacity of restraint that had been the traditional republican virtues of the *urbi et orbi* (Rome and the World). The dog is the first animal domesticated by man, the usually accepted prototype of fidelity and recognised legendary companion of man. The presence of the Dog and of the Scorpion has also been interpreted by some authors as symbols of the constellation that precede and follow the zodiacal sign of Mitra.

Ossanna reproduces a photo of a sculpture in the round now in the Vatican Museums, of a standing *leontocephalus* retrieved from the excavations done at Ostia, ancient Rome's main sea-port. This monstrous imaginary creature was perhaps produced by the fantasy of Romans in late BCE or early CE times. It shows the lion-headed, winged creature emerging from a rock holding a sceptre and keys in its hands, it has varying features in various Mithraea. Al-Biruni (full name: Abu al-Rayhan Muhammad ibn Ahmad al-Biruni, born on 4 September CE 973 in Chorasmia [Khwarizm], now Uzbekistan) quotes from the Purāṇas the myth of Narasiṁha the lion-headed human whose appearance on earth coincides with the evening *saṁdhi*, the moment in time that marks the passage from daylight to night darkness or vice versa from darkness to sunlight at dawn. Al-Biruni quotes the myth as an example of the importance given by "the Indians" to the measure of time and of the importance of determining the exact moment when the centre of the solar disc crosses the meridian of the place (*see* below, Appendix and Notes).[17]

Mythraea of all ages are found far and wide, from the Iberian peninsula in the West, to Egypt and Central Asia as far as ancient Persepolis in present-day southern Iran, from North Africa up to and beyond Hadrian's wall in Britain. Mithraea have been found in all the geographic areas where the legions of the late *Res publica,* the Republic of Rome (last century BCE) and those of the Roman Empire were stationed for some time.

In this essay we are not concerned with Mazdeism as a religion and culture. We are focused on Mitra (Mithra) as the God of Law and Justice, the God of treaties, pacts, agreements, fast and enduring friendship and fidelity. Our focus is on Mitra as an archetype as defined by Jung and sealed by the *dexterarum conjunctio* of Man with the Divine.

This short essay is also not the place to enter into details of the personality of the Iranian/Persian God Mithra since eminent scholars and historians studied the *Avesta* and Mithra in detail. However, most studies were isolated and totally alien to the Vedic and Vedāntic texts that are either repeatedly mentioned superficially and imperfectly or not at all. Some authors say that a god named Mitra is also mentioned in the *Ṛgveda* but ". . . only a single hymn is addressed to him" (Alberti, 2008, etc.), this is not correct. Mitra is called by name in about 275 hymns and in over 35 hymns as the dual Mitra/Varuṇau of the *Ṛgveda* alone and more often, specially in the *Avesta,* the God is present, addressed to indirectly or is referred to only by his attributes, as proper behaviour and good manners recommend.

Some recent publications, among them the recent book by Ossanna (1988), have traced back to the ancient I-E roots in Central Asia, namely the I-A and I-I whom we know well from the oral and written traditions (Vannucci, 2007; forthcoming), the personalities invoked, praised and revered in the theogony and theology of those people. Mitra as an Āditya is one of the founding stones of the culture and religion of all the Arya people of Central Asia. The ancient Āditya, the real *Mitr* is a true friend who has never abandoned each and everyone of us. Psychologically *Mitr* is the prototype of a living archetype (*fig.* 10).

This concise essay is only a brief approach to a study of the God in its Persian and post-Persian form, from the last century BCE and through the first half of the first millennium CE; it only looks briefly at the symbolism of the various forms of the Mithra-related iconography. This study is limited to the understanding of the early history of the personality of the Vedic Mitra, the God's evolution into the Persian Mithra and the spread of his religion and culture throughout the Roman Empire.

I would like to close this brief study quoting from Ossanna's (1998) well-informed and in-depth study of "the sense of Salvation in Mithraism" which is a study of the soteriological (*soteriology* is the doctrine of salvation) aspects of Mithraism, an oriental cult introduced in the Roman Empire. I quote from Ossanna (loc. cit.) (*fig.* 10).

> *The ultimate "mystery" of Mithraism is the concept of Salvation . . . but what salvation are we talking about? . . . (a) The salvation that is directly addressed to Man, to the followers and the faithful, to the habitat of Man, the Earth and the entire Cosmos . . . (b) What does Mithraism save us from?*

Summarising, I quote: (*a*) *it saves the Earth and the Cosmos from sterility and the dangers of death;* (*b*) *it saves the Cosmos, the Earth and man from error, lies and untruth, it brings sincerity, truth and mental light;* (*c*) *saves from mortality and ensures the eschatology of a happy life in heaven;* (*d*) *saves man from his own weakness, fear, uncertainty and a worthless life and makes of man a faithful and brave soldier;* (*e*) *saves man from internal disharmonies. . . .*

This conclusion evidently includes both the original lessons of Zarathustra and the later additions of fully developed Mithraism, as it entered and took root in the Roman Empire as a new-to-Rome religion, hence the emphasis on military virtues.

I would like to add a personal note. All men and women need the *dexterarum conjunctio,* also called the *dexiosis* or handclasp and what it represents to believe and have faith throughout their conscious and conscientious existence. Only this conviction will enable us to live bravely and without despair even as the vicissitudes of the act of living soar high and with overpowering suffocation. Faith in Mitra and what he represents helps us to remember that surviving is eternally a question of appropriate choices.

6

Summary and Conclusion

Mitra / Mithra / Mithraism

THE theology and theogony of the Vedas and of the *Avesta* are not explained in the ancient texts of India and Iran in the present sense of the verb "to explain." Nevertheless the essential thoughts and arguments of the ethical world of the ancient "books" were partially elaborated upon by Mazdeism in Persia and were developed further by the Vedānta and other philosophical schools in India. Mithraism is a well defined and specific, independent and unique shoot of the Vedic/Avestic world of thoughts, philosophy and religion. There is a direct line of development from the ancient common root of the I-A and I-I people, their beliefs, songs, hymns, religion and philosophies that is most clearly represented by the origin and evolution of God Mitra (Mithra), present in the Universe and begotten by Aditi who is herself or better, itself the representative of the Infinite, a fundamental Idea, Concept and Force. Mithraism is not an unwanted burden placed on man's shoulders and mind, it is instead a protective guardian and mental system symbolised by the *handclasp* or *dexiosis*, not to be confused or translated as the handshake of the Romans that has a different story and meaning behind it and is also physically a different sort of grasp.

The name of Vedic God Mitra may be traced back to the I-E idea and notion of Measure, Proportions, Law, Order and Might. In an earlier paper (Vannucci, 1998) I showed that the roots of the cult of Goddess Demeter in Attica, particularly at Athens, are to be found in Central Asia. Demeter arrived in Attica towards the middle of the second millennium BCE, during the reign of the first (?) King Pandion of Athens. Goddess Demeter was foremost the symbol of an agricultural deity who introduced superior varieties of wheat in Greece and taught the correct manner for raising crops in tune with the yearly cycle of the seasons of that geographic region. Later in Rome, as the complexities of the developing cultures and growing human population required, Demetra (Demeter) acquired also the role of legislator, regulator and judge in matters such as the use of the *ager* (land, soil, country) for the benefit of all, peasants and owners of the fields and for increase of more and better produce by agriculture. Demetra is therefore, as her name also indicates, the goddess of measure, law and order in agriculture, in the ancient Graeco-Roman world. The "career" or evolution of the history of Demeter repeats, but is not identical with the original and earlier history of God Mitra of the Vedas and of Mithra of the *Avesta* and later with Mazdeism to a limited extent.

The culture of both the I-A and the Indo-Iranians evolved as elsewhere, from nomadic pastoralism to partially or completely settled farming usually associated to transhumance. Consequently also the cultic and philosophic aspects of the religion and liturgy evolved and became more complex over time. Among the I-A Mitra becomes diversified into the personification of several deities whose attributes and functions (Greek *timaì* or *timé*) are adjusted to the complexities of settled living, of urbanisation and of the development of major hydrological studies and prospects, irrigation, hydraulic or sewerage works. All of these are cause and consequence of extensive agriculture, stock breeding, local and distant trade, complex administration and justice, travel by land, sea and rivers. In the *Avesta*, and with the advent of Zarathustra, Mithra remains the foremost Judge, Lawgiver and Preserver of Order and of the new religion better called Mazdeism. The basic characteristics of Mithraism as a religious movement, was the development and acceptance of this new religion that followed Mazdeism and flourished since the middle of the last century BCE in Rome and throughout the Roman Empire and in the Sassanid period in Central Asia. Mazdeism and Ahura-Mazda vanish with the introduction of Mithraism in Rome and the Roman Empire at large.

The I-A God Mitra is limited by *pāśa*s (fetters), that are the symbol and definition of his attributes and field of action. Mitra was the second "son" of Aditi (neutral in Sanskrit), is the personification of the concept of Infinite or *never-ending* like the sky whose limits are unknown and the circle itself where every single point is both the end of a cycle and the beginning of another. Mitra's antiquity is attested by his own nature and he is rooted as an archetype present in man's psyche. The basic attributes of Mitra, his *timai* could be described, or defined with just a few words: *Friendship, Trust, Fidelity, Loyalty, Honesty* and above all *Reason.* Mitra and his world are all this, he is the first, the mightiest, the wonderful support of Man, taken individually and/or collectively. Throughout his evolution Mitra is not specifically deified, though he is associated to the Great Splendour that is the Sun, as a partner of the *duo* Sūrya/Savitr̥. Mitra becomes inevitably and intrinsically associated with the principle, the order, the regularity and essence of the great splendorous might that is Ahura-Mazda. In late iconography Mitra as *Mithra* (also *Mithria*) is often represented with a halo of sunrays usually placed behind his head and by the eternal, indelible handclasp with Sūrya-Savitr̥ in the Vedas, or with Ahura-Mazda in the *Avesta* and following texts of Mazdeism. Finally Vedic Mitra is more forcibly and often invoked and praised together with the mighty, great and splendid Savitr̥ who is Pure Essence and Energy. He is represented as such in the Gāyatrī *mantra*.

The earliest records that have come down to us are to be read in the *Ṛgveda* where we see Mitra associated to Varuṇa, the first and only unfettered "son" of Aditi. The two Ādityas complement one another, together they uphold The Law and Rule of Earth and Sky. They are guardians of cultic practices, rites and rituals, they punish sin, untruth and bad or wicked behaviour. They reward Goodness, Correct behaviour and Obeisance to The Law throughout the Vedas (*ṚV* I; II.89; III.59.9, etc.). They are mighty and powerful, hence they are also addressed as kings who maintain the Law of the Universe, personified by Aditi. They give protection to man "with all aids that make him rich." In a late hymn Mitra is invoked as the god "who stimulates man to work, who sustains earth and sky, prepares the oil for the oblations, frees man from sickness, wounds or fear," in addition to being the God who *sustains the sacred Law*. The last steps of the career of God Mitra are entombed in the Mithraea.

The personality of Mitra evolves and adapts to changing times. In Rome, from the middle of the last century BCE, the cult of Mithra was gradually absorbed by the military, specially the officers of the Roman legions who had been trained to obey and give unconditional support to the Emperor and the Empire. Already Julius Caesar (100-44 BCE) insisted in being called *divo*, the first step towards the later habitual appellation of the "divine" Roman emperors.

Historically the personality of Mitra evolves in tune with ecological and cultural diversification, growing complexity and increase in knowledge of the various groups of people who worshipped Mitra, Mithra the Sublime Judge. This is how Mitra was and survives as "Measure and Proportions," the ground and cornerstone of civilised societies. Unfortunately present-day lifestyle of so-called civilised societies are running too fast to care about "measure = Mitra" and because of lack of the sense of measure and proportions modern societies only too often trip over their own feet.

Finally I would point out that one of the most interesting results of the present study is the finding that in terms of philosophy there is an unquestionable identity between Mitra's lion-headed man called *leontocephalus* as represented in the Roman Mithraea, and Narasiṁha, the man-lion of the Hiraṇyakaśipu myth as told in the *Bhāgavata Purāṇa* and explained in the *Īśa Upaniṣad* (*see* S. Radhakrishnan, 1953, 1974).

There have been lengthy discussions by learned scholars on the personality of the Vedic God Mitra, alternately called Mithra and his evolution over time and through several alien cultures superimposed on the original Vedic Mitra. At this stage I will draw the curtain because of my human limitations though the subject matter will never be closed. With the growing complexities and demands made upon those of us who try to go on living at peace with our conscience, meditation on God Mitra is a great help. There is a lengthy literature in a variety of languages and I anticipate that it will continue to grow because Mitra or Mithra as an archetype, whether called Narasiṁha or *leontocephalus* cannot be but everlasting. Mitra is and will be alive as long as Man as a species will be alive in spite of the continuous effort from all quarters to *beastialize* (apologies for this personal neologism from the adjective *beastly*) this same man in spite of the many venerable sages and wise men who have tried and still try to teach us that there are better ways to "make a living" than many of those practised at present.

Mitra/Mithra/Mythra is present as an intelligent and conscious Being in all aspects and facts of Life and Living since the origin of Man. Mitra is present throughout the evolution and development of all cultures as the ideal Friend. I close quoting from *ṚV* X.191 (Ṛṣi Saṁvanana, and from the *Atharvaveda* VI.64) which is an invocation to Agni, the sacred

Fire-god who illuminates conceptually and literally the general assembly of the people. This is most probably the last hymn of the *Ṛgveda,* it refers to the *saṁjñānam,* the general assembly called of all the clans when important decisions had to be taken.

1. Thou, mighty Agni gatherest up all that is precious for thy friend [*Mitra*]

   Bring us all the treasures as thou art enkindled in libation's place

2. Assemble, speak together: let your minds be all of one accord

   As ancient Gods unanimous sit down to their appointed share

3. The place is common, common the assembly, common the mind, so be their thought united

   A common purpose do I lay before you, and worship with your general oblation

4. One and the same be your resolve, and be your minds of one accord

5. United be the thoughts of all that all may happily agree

— Tr. Griffith

Appendix

FROM al-Biruni's: *Kitab tahqiq ma li'l-Hind min maqula maqbula fi'l-'aql aw mardula* — tr. from original Arabic by Giorgio De Martino, in: G. Bezza, *Gli astri il tempo il mondo*, 1997, (edn. Xenia).[17]

The title of chapter number eight of al-Biruni's book is "The Pole of the Sky" (al-Biruni, 1997; also Mazumdar, 2005). The second paragraph begins with the sentence: "I have heard a single tale about the South Pole. It is about a *daitya* king whose name was Uttānapāda. He had a very young son called Dhruv (Dhruva, immobile, permanent) who was a staunch devotee of Viṣṇu and had his mind constantly fixed on God. Dhruv went through severe penances until he was granted that after becoming a great king he would be rewarded for his one-minded steady faith in God. This is how Dhruv was immortalised as the Pole Star after he passed away.

Another Purāṇa tale quoted by al-Biruni is about king Hiraṇyakaśipu who deserved to dwell in heaven but he would not accept the idea of giving up the body when his soul would leave it. Hiraṇyakaśipu was a very powerful *asura* and even the gods had succumbed to him and were running away from heaven. Hiraṇyakaśipu had a young son called Prahlāda who was a great devotee of Viṣṇu. His father called him one day to enquire what he was studying and the boy replied by singing praises to Viṣṇu, the Supreme Deity. Hiraṇyakaśipu was jealous and very angry but Prahlāda would continue to maintain that Viṣṇu was the Supreme God. Hiraṇyakaśipu ordered the teachers to take Prahlāda and teach him not to praise the *devas*, but Prahlāda never swerved from the path of truth and continued to sing praises to Viṣṇu. The king ordered the child to be killed, but no harm came to him as he was protected by Viṣṇu. Neither the bite of poisonous snakes, nor the weight of the elephant's heavy foot or the flames of fire could do any harm to Prahlāda. King Hiraṇyakaśipu believed that he was himself immortal as he had obtained a boon from Brahmā according to which he could not be killed by anyone or anything created by Brahmā, nor would he be killed either during day or night, neither outside nor inside a house, neither on land, sea or sky nor by any lifeless implements dry or wet (from Mazumdar, from *Viṣṇu Purāṇa* II.34). One day when the boy was in a court in front of a pillar singing the praises of Viṣṇu, Hiraṇyakaśipu rushed towards him asking: "Where is this Viṣṇu of yours whom you are always praising?" — "He is everywhere, in everyone and in everything! — "Let me see him in this pillar then" exclaimed the father raising his sword to kill Prahlāda. At that moment emerged from the pillar a monster with a human body and the head of a lion, Narasiṁha (man-lion). Then Hiraṇyakaśipu rushed at it with a mace in his hands and Viṣṇu in the form of Narasiṁha, caught hold of him on the doorstep of the house (neither inside nor outside) and setting him on his lap (neither on land, at sea nor in the sky) he tored it apart with his nails (neither with nor without life) and so ended the wicked Hiraṇyakaśipu.

The title of al-Biruni's chapter 21, is "Il *"saṁdhi,"* intervallo fra due tempi" [*Saṁdhi, the interval between two times*]. Here al-Biruni, (the Khwarizmian) refers to the meaning of the word *saṁdhi. Saṁdhi* is defined as the interval between day and night called crepuscule, or twilight and the interval between night and day, called daybreak or dawn and no other intervals of time are thus called. . . . The myth of Hiraṇyakaśipu and Praḥlāda is a metaphor used to define the meaning of the astronomical word *saṁdhi*. The word *saṁdhi* or *saṁdhya* (fem.) indicates the "conjunction of day and night, of morning and evening twilight

. . . (*apud* Anonymus, Glossario Sanskrito). The tale teaches how Prahlāda was saved by his steady conviction that God is everywhere. The story of Prahlāda, of Dhruv who was immortalised as the Pole Star (*Ursa Major*), of child Naciketas and his dialogue with Yamarāja ("king" of the deceased) and others also quoted by al-Biruni attest of the deep knowledge that the Khwarizmian astronomer had of Indian science and traditional knowledge that was told in the Purāṇas already many centuries before the birth of al-Biruni himself and of the expansion of scientific knowledge in Central Asia. The *leontocephalus* of the Roman Mithraea and Narasiṁha of the Purāṇas express the same concept, the emergence and development of human consciousness from the rocks, the bare earth, a concept discussed and defined by the oral tradition.

Going one step further, we may try to evaluate the meaning of the figure called *Mitra petragenus* (Mitra originated by the rocks, Mother Earth) frequently represented in the Mithraea. Mitra *petragenus* is rendered as a young boy emerging from the bare earth, his legs from the thigh down to the feet are still enclosed in the rocks. The *corax* (crow), the *nimphus* (also called *cripthus*) and the *miles* (soldier) are the symbols of the first three steps of the path leading to the initiation of the neophytes. The fourth step is *leo* (lion). The steps are always linked to each other in this order. The first three *avatāras* of Viṣṇu are the fish (*matsya)*, the tortoise (*kūrma*) and the boar (*varāha*). The fourth *avatāra* of Viṣṇu, the lion, corresponds to the lion (*narasiṁha*) of the fourth step taken by the neophytes initiated into the doctrine of the Roman Mithraea. The first three steps of initiation in the doctrine of Roman Mithraea correspond to the first three *avatāras* of Viṣṇu while the fourth is the same Narasiṁha as in the Vedic tradition. In either case the concept is the same: the evolution of life from primitive animals still living in water, the evolution of that creature up to the emergence of a Being conscious of having a conscience: Man. Though abridged, the two traditions, the Vedic and that shown in the Mithraea and validated by modern science, can be read as a shortened symbolic representation of the evolution of life forms on Earth as explained by contemporary studies on the appearance and evolution of animal life forms on Earth.

Notes

1. There is no possible answer to the question: "when did primitive man first develop the consciousness of being conscious?" It is reasonable to believe that primitive men had a conscience, a will and power of reason without which there would not have been mental and cultural developments of humankind. Psychologists, psychoanalysts, philosophers, psycho-physiologists and experimentalists have produced a variety of hypotheses that may have a kernel of truth but are equally difficult to prove or disprove. I have no competence in this matter and this would not be the place to discuss it. However, I wish to say that I strongly differ from authors who believe that "primitive man," whatever the meaning of the word "primitive," would be unable to perceive and even less have enough knowledge to express his thoughts on any philosophical topic such as consciousness and the measure of time, the order or chaos in the universe, his own existence and his place in the world he lived in or the existence of supernatural powers and so on. Man would be unable to think in terms of *eternal* or *infinite*, the *universe, space* and *time.* These notions would only be the product of developing intelligence, growing technical and intellectual knowledge and expertise along a process involving many generations. On the contrary I believe that primitive man or *Homo habilis* would be in a better position to gain the perception of what has been called *"Truth"*, *ṛta* in Sanskrit and *Est* (what *IS*) in Latin, or immanent reality of the physical and metaphysical worlds. I believe that ancient men and women and above all children were in a better position than modern man to feel with their senses and mind the realities of the tangible world into which they evolved. Modern man, unlike his "primitive" ancestors, is fenced away from Nature that *"is what is"* or *"quisquis es"* by his Ego and arrogance, by his own great inventions and complex man-made artificialities. Modern man is isolated away from the reality of Nature by his brain children, artificial lights whose glare hides away moon and

stars and by artificial sounds that cancel the "harmony of the spheres" (remember Plato, 427-347 BCE) and man-made monsters that are meant to "improve the quality of life" but create instead a world mostly unreal, fantastic and volatile. Most of the time modern men and women, and to a greater degree youth, are plunged into a virtual world more distracting than the labyrinth of the Minotaur of Crete. So-called "primitive man" could feel in his own body different types of energy, the pull of gravity, the rhythms of the seasons, of day and night, the rhythms of sounds, odours and perfumes which he shared with other living beings, plants, animals and microbes. Correctly pronounced classical Sanskrit is pure music, a precious relict from ages past. There is little archaeological or documentary evidence of sounds, except for correctly chanted Sanskrit and relics of sounds of ancient voices. There is at present little evidence of the use and meaning of sounds and music from the early stages of the acculturation of man. Ancient man was undoubtedly nearer and closer to gods and had a better developed extrasensory perception of the world he lived in than present-day highly learned persons, men or women. Children are more sensitive than adults, but urban education takes care to suffocate as early as possible constructive innate archetype images not suitable or not necessary to turn a child into a "winner" in the contemporary destructive world. Even breastfeeding of one's infant has been considered undesirable since "industrially produced formulas are more appropriate for the baby than mother's milk because they are the result of scientific research"! These and other hundreds of similar sentences run into illogical circles or fall in the abyss of Dante's Inferno. C.J. Jung (first publ. 1961, here quoted it. ed. BUR, 2006 pp. 233, 353, 357) was interested in the psychology of primitive men, and frequently touched this subject in his papers, books, lectures and discussions; however he never completed a manuscript on the psychology of the Pueblo Indians of New Mexico. In the Introduction to his Autobiography (l.c., pp. 27ff.) Jung ponders on what it means to be a man. The master answers the question with the statement of his inner conviction: ". . . the same as all other *beings*" (italic mine) "same as fragment of the Infinite Godhead."

2. *Ṛgveda* I.2.7/9 is a relatively late hymn that reads in Griffith's translation

   7. Mitra, of holy strength, I call, and foe-destroying Varuṇa, Who made the oil-fed rite complete

8. Mitra and Varuṇa, through the Law, lovers and cherishers of Law
   Have ye obtained your mighty power.
9. Our Sages, Mitra-Varuṇa, of wide dominion, strong by birth,
   Vouchsafe us strength that worketh well.

— Ṛṣi Madhucchandaas, tr. Griffith

The word "Law" here means *ṛta* that *"is what IS."* Copying from note 7, p. 2 of Griffith: "According to Sāyaṇa, Mitra presides over the day as Varuṇa over the night: hence the closest connection subsists between the two deities who are more frequently invoked together than Varuṇa is invoked singly. Together they uphold and rule the earth and sky, together they guard the world, together they promote religious rites, avenge sin, and are the lords of truth and light." "Through the Law: i.e. in accordance with *ṛta,* the eternal law or everlasting rule of the universe." *Ṛgveda* I.1.8 reads: *Ruler of sacrifice, guardian of Law eternal, radiant One* — Ṛta is everything in the universe that is imbued with Regularity of Action. After the *praṇava,* in transliteration the Gāyatrī *mantra* reads:

"aum bhūr bhuvaḥ svaḥ tat savitur vareṇyam
bhargo devasya dhīmahi dhiyo yo naḥ pracodayāt

and in translation the verse could be rendered:

— We shall meditate on the Glory, the Splendour and the Grace that emanate from that Light

— May we reach final liberation by the awakening of the innate intelligence that pervades the universe.

3. Basically Mitra shares with man the agonistic eagerness to learn, to know and understand always more. None could fulfil this task better than Mitra who is the measure of everything material and spiritual. Later, Savitṛ was personified as the "essence . . . or idea/ concept of the Sun" who sees everything that happens on Earth and proceeds assiduously on its basic assignment: to ensure the strictly observed periodic recurrence of the astral bodies and to survey Order in the Cosmos. The same orders are alive and are entered into the musical chanting of the *mantras* that regulate classic Sanskrit into perfect harmony. — *Ṛgveda* VIII; Vālakhylya IV.3

   He to whom Viṣṇu came striding his three wide steps, as Mitra's statutes ordered it — Ṛṣi Srustigu, tr. Griffith

   Mitra, a typical archetype in terms of Jung's terminology, is also one of the most ancient Vedic gods. Mitra represents the rationalisation of the vital association and participation of man with nature as well as the need to give respect and obeisance, recognition and all that needs to be acknowledged and offered to the Powers beyond Man's physical, mental and intellectual capacity, because this is their due. As a friend of mine put it: "My concept of God is that God is the sum total of all the known Laws of Nature plus and specially so, the yet unknown Laws."

4. Bhargava (2001: 69, note 38) clarifies that "The words Āditya and Daitya are formed from Aditi (Infinity) and Diti (Finiteness) respectively by the addition of the affix *nya* . . . "The word *daitya* is simply an antonym of "Aditi" preceded by the negative *a*. In the course of time and in the Purāṇic period the words *dānava* and *daitya* acquired the meaning of demons. Similarly the name of Varuṇa changed into *asura* and retained the ancient meaning of a being imbued with great magical power.

5. The syllable *vā* or *vsa* meaning "free; to be empty" here means: "the great, large universe; space" (*see* Devoto 1968). As a personal side I would mention that when I lived in Kochi, Kerala, no person whose mother language was Malayalam could pronounce my name Vannucci as in Italian, my mother tongue. The letter *v* was pronounced like *ua*, like English *w*. According to most etymologists *wa* is the original I-E pronunciation of the syllable.

6. In the *Ṛgveda*, Mitra and Varuṇa are called *deva*s (gods), *asura*s (mighty) and *samrāja* (kings, universal kings), (*Ṛgveda*; VIII. 25.4/8 and *Ṛgveda* VIII. 59) and kṣatriyas (rulers, kings) also in *ṚV*. VIII. 67, (sovereigns) and elsewhere. Gods are energisers and should not only be worshipped, they should also be obeyed. Because the knowledge and wisdom of the first gods was recognised, admitted and understood by the *ṛṣi*s they must be forever followed for man's own safety, welfare and happiness (*Ṛgveda* I.24/1)

   (1) Who now is he, what God among Immortals,
   of whose auspicious name we may bethink us?
   Who shall to mighty Aditi restore us.
   That I may see my Father and my Mother?

   — Ṛṣi Sunahshepa, tr. Griffith

   (2) From *Ṛgveda* III.59/9
   Mitra to Gods, to living man, to him who strews the holy grass
   Gives food fulfilling the sacred Law

   — Ṛṣi Viśvāmitra, tr. Griffith

The ground where rites and rituals or any and all sacrifices would take place is beforehand "purified" by sprinkling water and scattering fragments of one or more than one of the sacred grasses over the area. The most auspicious is the *kuśa* grass. Any meaningful symbolic act of physical purification of a place that will be the appropriate site for the hoped for spiritual purification to be reached through meditation and concentration of the mind, must be purified to fulfil the sacred Law.

7. Jung (first publ. 1912; Its reprint 2006, p. 49) mentions that when he was carrying out preliminary studies for his book *Wandlungen und Symbole des Libido* [in Italian tr.: Trasformazioni e simboli della libido (2006)] he suddenly realised that "there are archaic psychic elements that have entered into the individual psyche through channels other than tradition . . ." (l.c., p. 121) ". . . I saw myself in a dream carrying a little light in the midst of a foggy storm in a dark night and in a place unknown to me . . . and I realised that the small light was indeed my conscience and that was the only light I had." In another context (l.c., p. 171) Jung says that ". . . since 1909 I realised that I would not be able to cure [*patients with latent*] psychotic conditions unless I could decipher their symbolism. It was then that I began to study mythologies . . . not with the purpose of confirming a theory but because it is indeed the patient who must learn to know himself as an individual." . . . "This however can be achieved only when it is seen in connection with the "collective unconscious [*concepts of the people at large*]." It is from this perspective and following Jung's teachings that I have made an attempt to understand the Mitra/Varuṇa relationship, later represented by the Mitra (Mitra/Sun/Savitṛ relationship) and Mithra/Ahura-Mazda relationship symbolised by the *dexiosis* or *dexterarum conjunctio.* Ahura-Mazda is the Supreme Being [*the good principle*] of Mazdeism, latter known in the West as Zoroastrianism. In Vedism the Gāyatrī *mantra* is its idealised representation that recalls this relationship with all its implications for the welfare of the individual and the community (*Ṛgveda* III. 62.10/11, *see also Note* 2 above).

8. Mitra is said *invictus, de petra natus* (born invincible from the rocks) and the rocks are in turn said *petra genetrix* (rocks or soil as generators). "In late iconography Mithra is shown as a newborn infant boy emerging from the rocks with a Phrygian cap on his head, a dagger in the right hand and what is seen by Ossanna (1988) as a flaming torch in the left. The "flaming torch" could perhaps be interpreted as a *barsom* that was traditionally made of a bunch of twigs tied together. The sculpture is in low relief, somewhat weathered and

not very clear. The original is kept in the Musei Capitolini, Rome. Ossanna also gives the photo of a sculpture in the round figuring a *leontocephalus* from the Vatican Museum, Rome, that appears wound up by what could be the coils of a long and heavy serpent. Both the newborn infant and the *leontocephalus* are fruits of late developments of the Mitra cult, after the god had become Mithra. The first figure represents the birth of the god from generous Mother Earth and is called *Mitra petragenus* (born from the rocks). The second shows the hideous figure of a being wound up by a serpent that could represent the fetters with which Varuṇa encircles and punishes the wrong-doers. The lion-headed monster has been variously interpreted by authors ancient and modern. The *leontocephalus* obviously represents a punishment or execution and I would look at it as giving a forecast or warning of what may happen to anyone who defies the holy laws guarded by Mithra. The *leontocephalus* is an emblem of the duo Mitra/Varuṇa where Mitra formulates the judgement and Varuṇa executes the punishment. It may be read as having the same meaning and sentiments that cause the gradual degradation of the features of the painting of Oscar Wilde's hero as he practises one evil act after another in *The Picture of Dorian Grey*. Unlike Mitra, Varuṇa over the centuries and millennia does not become diversified into various specialised gods, Varuṇa the God becomes ever greater, imbued with the eternal principle of goodness and wisdom named Ahura-Mazda. Varuṇa grows as the personification of Light, Warmth, Splendour, Power or, in modern terms, Infinite Energy. Varuṇa as Ahura-Mazda impersonates the Power and Energy that create and sustain Life; Solar Energy and Heat that put in motion photosynthesis and the atmospheric water cycle. At the end of his travels through Hell and Purgatory, Dante expresses the same concept with the following words: "Love that moves the Sun and other Stars."

9. Bhargava (2001: 61-65) gives well documented arguments taken from the *Ṛgveda* and from the *Avesta* to explain the exchange of qualifications of the names and attributes of deities mentioned in Vedism and in Avestism. I quote from Bhargava (l.c.) ". . . that the words *deva* and *asura* began to be used in the opposite sense by the two sections of the Aryas" . . . "is proved by the later Purāṇic literature. A conflict between two sectors of the Aryan kings and *ṛṣis* . . . The Ṛgvedic gods underwent four main types of changes in the Purāṇas as well as in the *Avesta* . . . Varuṇa's chief epithets *asura* and *medhira* became the name of the Iranian Supreme God under

the form of Ahura-Mazda. . . . All these [*and many more*] are strong proofs of the fact that the separation of the Iranians and the Indians took place after the composition of the bulk of the *Ṛgveda*." Quoting from Ossanna (1988: 33), Vedic Mitra and Varuṇa become the two immortal benefactors of Ahura-Mazda in the Avestic period of Zarathustra. Ahura-Mazda is the Supreme God while Mitra is the God with the authority and power of the Judge and Regulator of testaments and contracts. Following Alberti (2008), the word *ahura* comes from the ancient Avestic word *anshu* meaning: "Breath of Life, world, God, Lord." The word is related to the word *ansu*=spirit, and old Germanic *ansuz*, a divine lineage of the Nordic mythology. *Ahura* means: Lord, Creator of life, "the one who creates just with his thought," or: "the one whose thought alone can create." The word *mazda* is related to the I-E root *mendh*, that in Greek means "to learn." Dandamayev (1996, *fig*. 7) reproduces the imprint of an Achaemenid cylinder seal with the name of Darius. The caption is in cuneiform script and the language presumably Aramaic. The *figure* shows Darius hunting lions, one of them lying dead under the galloping horses and another standing on its rear legs with two kingly arrows stuck in its forehead and chest. The figure is specially significant as it gives dates and technical details of the chariot with its eight-spoke wheels and of the harnessing of the horse, of the charioteer and of two date-palm trees. What is particularly interesting from the present point of view is that the figure is historically dated and the image of the mighty Ahura-Mazda with extended wings looms large over the head of the king, it exhibits in detail all the attributes of Splendour and Might typical of the Great Protector Ahura-Mazda as well as that of the great human king Darius.

10. Ahura-Mazda is frequently represented in stereotypical form in the Achaemenid period either in front or side view, always with the wings fully extended. In the Sassanid and Kuṣāṇa-Sassanid periods, Mithra and the Sun are gradually more rarely represented. Mitra, as the great friend, as Measure and Justice, as the Sun, Life and Amity is often represented associated to Sūrya in the *dexiosis* or *dexterarum conjunctio*, the handclasp of Mithra with the Sun. In the Mithraea, God Mithra may be shown together with all the signs of the zodiac, meaning that the association is everlasting. The images of Mithra in the Roman period usually show an enthusiastic adolescent or still beardless young man performing the ritual killing of the bull (*tauroctony*) *figs*. 9, 10 while in the formal images of the

dexiosis the two gods, Mithra and Sūrya are extremely serious and mature masculine figures performing the ceremony with godly austerity as equals. Much has been written about the meaning of the *dexiosis* and about the relationship of Mithra with the Sun-God. In Vedism Mitra is a God who represents Man and is his advocate at important functions such as the sealing of pacts. Mitra greets the Sun or Sūrya as a heavenly body and greets him also as Savitṛ the luminous and numinous god. The *dexiosis* is a development of the iconography of the two gods, it symbolises the unbreakable alliance between Mithra as a man with the two astral bodies: Sūrya and Savitṛ the essence or God of Great Splendour. Mitra/Sūrya and Mitra/Savitṛ are restrained by ethical limitations, the fetters, as all the Ādityas, except Varuṇa, are also restrained, though they exist since the origin of time. The *dexiosis* is an understanding, a sacred oath, a profession of Faith, an unbreakable Pact of Honesty, of correct Thoughts and Acts, of Friendship and Love and all that makes Life good and ethically correct. The *dexiosis* symbolises the integration of physical Man who is limited though rational, with the spiritual Being, infinite and eternal. It is a symbol of perfect harmony, of perfect resonance between body and soul, or in Jung's terms, between the I and the Selbst. This is the ideal aim that is always sought but never completely achieved by man on Earth.

11. These matters bring to mind the five "Regular Polyhedrons" built by Plato (427-347 BCE) based on Euclidean geometry. The five regular polyhedrons are each limited by the sphere that contains and sustains them. All the angles of the polyhedrons touch the inner surface of the sphere, thus they are all perfectly circumscribed by the sphere itself. It is geometrically proven that there cannot be more than five regular polyhedrons circumscribed by a sphere, but there are or may be produced an infinite number of *non-regular* polyhedrons that are not perfectly and entirely included by a sphere. It is also well known that Plato considered that four basic elements, earth, water, air and fire were used by the Demiurge as building blocks to put order in the primaeval chaos and thereby build and put the World in mathematical order and therefore in functional state. In a similar abridged manner we may say that the ancient *ṛṣis*, based on their observation of Nature and using Reason expressed a similar idea or knowledge in a different manner than Plato. However all these philosophers, in the Greek sense of the word, arrived at comparable conclusions about the unchanging and therefore "eternal" Laws of Nature. By different routes, they

acquired an "understanding" of the essential aspects of the Absolute Truth on which they built their mental representation and tentative explanations. Plato had the following warning carved on the entrance to *his* Academia: "Do not enter if you are not a geometer."

12. There is no doubt that Mithraism was introduced in Rome towards the middle of the last century BCE. It is also well established that the new cult came from Asia Minor and more specifically from Anatolia and that it is an offshoot of the ancient religion/philosophy of the I-A and I-I of Central Asia who moved westwards along the northern regions of the Asia Minor peninsula, coming from the river Gorgan plains, south-east of the Caspian Sea and from surrounding areas, [Vannucci (forthcoming)]. The infiltration of the I-A into the western foreign lands was gradual and involved a small amount of people, while the bulk of the population of Mitanni and of the Hittite kingdoms was mostly Hurrian. The Hurrians were mountain people coming mostly from the Zagros mountains. The movement westwards of the I-A clans was not the result of sudden enthusiastic expansionism, it continued for an unspecified period of time, during decades or few centuries. In the context of this brief essay it would be futile to search whether the incoming nomads included or not both I-A and I-I clans because the pre-Zoroastrian gods and religion were the same. Most authors believe that the Vedic I-A were the first to move into Anatolia as suggested by the gods which they took with them. As mentioned in the text, the most important were the primaeval Ādityas (Varuṇa, Mitra, Bhaga, Aryamān and the two Aśvins (Twins)) to which Indra was added later, according to the oral tradition, history and later recorded documents. The "king" [of man and gods] also called God Indra and his faithful followers, *"the Maruts, originally storm gods, warrior gods, Indra's friends and associates, proud receivers of soma libations . . ."* (Chakravarty, 1997) came along, riding their horses and driving their chariots. The Maruts are called *maryaḥ* (*Ṛgveda* I. 64.2 – VII. 56.1) and "sons of Rudra (*Ṛgveda* V. 59.6) and *maryannu* in later songs, myths and invocations. Liverani (2009) and other authors quote the *maryannu* as *"mounted horsemen"* who had received special weapons and training. There is no doubt that the use of the horse in peace and war in Western Asia began or was enhanced only after the arrival of the I-A whether mixed or not with I-I. From the point of view of this concise study the important point is that the dates of the first kings of the kingdom of Hatti are well known, as well as the relationship between the king and his *maryannu* (approximate

meaning: *boisterous young men*, always ready to fight for Indra). The first well-established kings of the ancient kingdom of Hatti were Hattusili 1st and Murishili 1st who lived in the middle sixteenth to fifteenth centuries BCE. The much spoken-of teachings and the treatise on horse training by a now famous man called Kikkuli also belongs to this period. The God Mitra is present during the period of expansion of the well-organised Hittite kingdom and the conquest of Babylon, dated 1531 BCE. Chakravarty (1997) points out that both Indra and the Maruts have all the characteristics of euhemeristic deities because of their decisive role in the expansion and establishment of the Indo-Aryans over vast geographic areas of Central Asia and for the protection and service they offer to mankind. Stretching this further, we could find a resemblance between the social and political function of Indra with his *vajra*, his chariot with the pair of horses (the *haris*) and his faithful Maruts (*maryaḥ*) with the Italian "condottieri" leading their groups of mercenaries in the Middle Ages and the Renaissance, and even more so with the figure of the French Godfrey of Bouillon (CE 1061?-1100), who led the first Crusade to *"the Holy Land"* for the *"liberation of the Saint Sepulchre of Jesus Christ."* Chrakravarty (1997) also shows that the role and status of the Maruts with the passage of centuries became gradually less important during the performance of rituals. Presumably this would have happened when the age of expansionism was over and was followed by permanent settlements and different lifestyles. Indra however maintains forever the full glory of the great leader, even when there was no longer need of the support of the Maruts whose help had been required in the early times of geographical expansion but was no longer required because of the long-drawn peaceful infiltration of the I-A among the local predominant populations of Hurrians and other locals. The religious tolerance of the Hittites and peaceful cultural exchanges with their neighbours is well known, while the presence of the bellicose leader Indra and his *Indra-jyesṭhaḥ* (Indra's people) also decreases among the western I-A populations. In late Vedic literature the Maruts are called *devaviṣaḥ* (subjects of the gods) and Chakravarty considers them to be *nature anthropomorphised*. Except for Mitra and Sūrya, the Sun, the original I-A or I-I deities are absent as such when Mithraism enters in Rome, but nevertheless their cultural traits and qualifications may be readily identified. A close analysis of parts of some of the Brāhmaṇas, specially the *Śatapatha* and the *Aitareya Brāhamaṇa* lead towards this interpretation.

13. Ossanna (l.c., p. 32) discusses at length the opinion of earlier authors on the relationship between Mitra/Mithra and the Sun as well as other details of the iconography and liturgy of the Mithraic Faith. The plan and basic arrangement of the temples is the same everywhere but authors give varying readings about the meaning of the figures, of iconography and of the epigraphy of the Mithraea. Wherever we may still see original figures, general iconography or written texts we find that they invariably belong to a late period of the history of the cultural evolution of the original Vedic/Avestic gods. Outside India, most of the oral tradition was lost as is obvious also from the *Shah-Nameh* of Firdausi. The study of isolated figures of very ancient deities inevitably renders only imperfect or skewed readings to the eyes of modern man living under entirely different cultural conditions. This is not the place to review the extensive literature on the matter, the salient point in the present context is that the relationship between Mitr/Mitra/Mithra and the Sun-God Sūrya-Savitṛ/Ahura-Mazda changes over the many centuries that followed the Vedic origin of the god. It also changes in the last transfer from the Iranian to the Roman Mithraism. What is enduring throughout the ages is that, again using Ossanna's terms, "there continues to be an active co-operation between the two gods" [Mithra and the Sun-God, whoever he is, *quisquis es*]. In the Roman period Mitra acquires a soteriological value because he offers salvation to mankind. Salvation may be achieved in different ways including by bloodshed, as the blood of the sacrificial bullock *that fertilises the soil.* Ossanna also points out that the essential point of the religion of Mithra is that *"cosmic reality" is present in the mithraeum and in the religion of Mithra . . . Mitra himself is "kosmocrator" because he has a cosmic function,"* namely to guarantee, to ensure that there is perfect harmony between Sky (or Heaven) and Earth. Mitra is the mediator between good and bad. There are also other basic features of Mithraism that are clearly expressed and discussed already in the Vedas and in the *Avesta*. The basic principles of the personality of Vedic God Mitra have survived down to present. Mitra is best appreciated not as an euhemeristic deity, but as an un-replaceable archetype of the personality called "the rational duo Man-Woman." This truth is manifest also by the inner urge of human beings to be reunited with the Infinite from where they come. This urge is variously interpreted and represented by different faiths but is universally recognised as the remembrance of the dead and of the innate respect for ancestors, for parents, as the attachment of the baby for its mother, of every normal person for its masters, teachers, saints and all those

who ensure the survival of the many virtual and immaterial realities worth living for present in the mind and psyche of the living person. One such immaterial reality, in the context of this short essay is the concept of Perfect Goodness, the Mithra/Ahura-Mazda might. It can give a sense of eternity to human beings.

14. The figure of prince Rāma, later king Rāma of Ayodhyā, the protagonist of the *Rāmāyaṇa* is an explicit example of an adult man who can behave differently and even against his own nature and inner will at different times and situations. When young Rāma's wife Sītā was abducted by evil demon Rāvaṇa, Rāma won the promise from the monkey people to go with him to Laṅkā to save captive Sītā. The monkey tribe was under the rule of unscrupulous Bālin (Bāli or Vāli) who delayed departure enjoying a good time in the meanwhile. Rāma's friend, good Sugrīva brother of Bālin had been dethroned by his brother and was temporarily unable to follow Rāma to Laṅkā to retrieve the young captive, gentle Sītā. Rāma finally decides to shoot an arrow at Bālin and kill him. Rāma's act was doubly wrong in that he did not only kill the then ruling king of the monkeys, but did so from under cover of a tree. These two faults were hardly justifiable and could mar the honour of a kṣatriya prince, even though the purpose was a holy act of retrieval of the aggrieved wife of prince Rāma. Sugrīva then remembered his promise to Rāma and they all marched against Laṅkā, Sītā was restored and became the queen of Ayodhyā when Rāma eventually sat on the throne. What happened, however, was that the washerman of the city was overheard saying that it was not proper for a king to bring back home a wife who had been kept in captivity by another man for a long time. Now King Rāma was torn between the loyalty due to his people and kingdom and the loyalty and love for Sītā, his wife who had already gone unscathed through the trial of fire to prove her purity after her return to Ayodhyā together with Rāma. When he was still a prince Rāma had decided that his duty towards his wife had greater bearing than the inevitable fault of killing an unworthy person from under cover and not in open fight. Now Rāma was back at Ayodhyā and was a king, he must decide between keeping his beloved wife with him in spite of the washerman's blame or uphold the honour of the kingdom and of the king who he now was. Rāma decided to ban Sītā off to live in the forest. Sītā was received there and taken care of in the *āśrama* of Ṛṣi Vālmīki and in due time she gave birth to Rāma's twin sons Kuśa and Lava who were educated by Sage Vālmīki himself in whose *āśrama* they

were born. Of course, Rāma was cleansed from his first foul act because he was still a young prince perhaps not mature enough to uphold kṣatriya *dharma* in open combat against a mischievous usurper. His duty and love for Sītā were strongest and the urge to retrieve her soonest, was a quick decision that had to be taken to proceed towards Laṅkā to save Sītā. The decision of the young prince to save his wife was correct, though at the cost of his honour. His second act when as a king he banned Sītā out of Ayodhyā was correct within the laws of *kṣātriya dharma* because the utmost duty of a king is towards his people and his kingdom whom he could not dishonour. Rāma took the best decisions considering the duties of a prince towards his wife and those of a king towards his people. Both decisions were painful for Rāma, arguments may be raised in favour or against them but they were taken consciously and they settled matters of vital importance in either case. This is how Mitra comes to our help when we must take decisions on big or small matters. Often all decisions are potentially correct and weigh on one's conscience, but unsettled matters are always the worse choice.

In connection to what I said above about twins that may represent the pairs of opposites on which we often stumble during a lifetime, I would further point out that Sītā gave birth to twins, while she was under the patronage and protection of one of the wisest *ṛṣis*, namely Vālmīki who is also the putative author of the *Rāmāyaṇa*. It is perhaps not an accident that Vālmikī introduces a pair of male twins as sons of a kṣatriya king who had to take extremely painful personal decisions to safeguard integrity, order and peace among his people.

15. Based on Greek mythology (the personality of Greek goddess Demeter (Demetra) and on historical data (the arrival of the goddess at Athens during the reign of one of the first Pandion kings, middle second millennium BCE), Vannucci (1988) suggested and offered arguments in favour of the origin of Goddess Demeter (Demetra) in Central Asia. Greek mythology says that the Goddess was brought to Greece by Heracles (Hercules) himself or by the men of the tribe of the Heraclides. In ancient Greece Demeter was credited with having brought to Attica the seeds of "bread wheat" that is an hexaploid variety of wheat: genetically characterised as AABBDD. Demeter also taught the correct agriculture of the new grains, she gave instructions about the division of the fields, cultivation of the new varieties, irrigation and other agricultural arts. Demeter entrusted the hierophant (highest priest of her first temple at Eleusis

near Athens) the secrets of the *patria* (the ancestral laws) that describe in detail all the laws and rules of ownership of the land, including the *cultic* aspects of the art new to Greece, though wheat was known in the northern borders of the Mediterranean Sea since a debatable length of time of several centuries earlier. What is known of the mysteries of Demeter is closely comparable with many of the rites and rituals of the cult of Mithra as practised in the Mithraea many centuries later, however discussions on the origin and name of the goddess are still alive among scholars (*see* Vannucci, l.c.). Following the same reasoning and reading over again the ancient literature, specially the "Dionysiacs" of Nonnos of Panopolis, the notes of the Orphic hymns, the Homeric hymns and later Roman authors, it is reasonable to accept the date of the arrival of Demeter in Attica during the kingdom of the first Pandion king, around the fifth or sixth centuries BCE an approximate timing that is also confirmed by palynological data. The story of Demeter is one of the many well known that confirm the cultural exchanges due to trade or war between Central Asia and the Mediterranean civilisations. The name of Goddess Demeter (Demetra) has been a source of lengthy debates and scholars have not arrived at a firm conclusion as far as I know. However, the affinity between De-metra, Meter/Mitra and God Mitra is obvious and they suggest a common origin in the name of God Mitra, meaning order, measure, law, justice, prosperity and correct proportions.

16. As mentioned in the text the importance of sound and music in the process of acculturation of man cannot be overemphasised. The *oṁkāra* (*Auṁ* or *Oṁ*), represents and includes all sounds, including vital breath and silence that is the absence of sound. The language of the I-A developed early and reached a high level of grammatical precision of what is now called classical Sanskrit. On the other hand, iconography was born late and underwent interaction with alien cultures, specially during the time of expansion of Hellenised cultures in Central Asia. Present and modern representations of Lord Śiva-Naṭarāja's *tāṇḍava* dance that put in motion the eternal cycle of the manifestation, transformation and decomposition of the cosmos, show Lord Śiva dancing over and controlling *kāla* (time) under his feet and with the *ḍamaru* (the clessidra-shaped small drum) in his lifted right hand. The *ḍamaru* represents the primordial sound (*nāda*) of all phenomena. The *tāṇḍava* dance itself represents the unending creation, conservation and transformation of the universe through sound, rhythm, movement and harmony. Time

(*kāla*) under the feet of the dancing Naṭarāja is shown as a young dwarf or better, as an ageless eternal creature. All details of the correct representation of Śiva Naṭarāja are based on the science of numerology and philosophical ideas and concepts. As an aside, I would recall that A.L. Lavoisier (1743-94), French pioneer chemist demonstrated scientifically the same principle saying: "In nature nothing is created, nothing is destroyed but everything is transformed." This is known as Lavoisier's principle or the Principle of Conservation of matter. Lavoisier was sent to the guillotine under the ignorant verdict: "La République n'a pas besoin de chimie" (the Republic has no use of chemistry).

17. Abu al-Rayhan Muhammad ibn Ahmad al-Biruni, was born on September 973 — d. 13 December CE 1048, in the city of Kaath in Chorasmia (Khwarizm, now Uzbekistan), in a family of Iranian origin. Al-Biruni was conversant with Persian, Sanskrit and other contemporary languages and scripts and had a good knowledge of Greek, Syrian and Hebrew. He was particularly interested in astronomy, physics and mathematics, subjects that he studied in depth preferably in the original languages. He translates the word *veda*, he spells *bidh* from the root to perceive, to know, to believe to be true, which I would translate as *co-gnoscere* (= Italian conoscere) meaning: to know, to see together, to share the knowledge of . . .; to be conscious of . . . . Al-Biruni was familiar with the Indian culture that he studied in-depth to the point of saying that "it is very difficult to enter into the Indian thought and their way of expressing their knowledge and reasons." The writings of Al-Biruni are a precious source of information on India, its science and scientists. He was the first non-Indian scientist who thoroughly studied the ancient philosophical and religious Indian texts and recognised that "Indians are not idolaters and Hinduism is fundamentally a monotheistic religion." Al-Biruni discusses impartially the convictions of Indian scientists and disagrees on some points, such as "The Indians insist (believe) that *matter* exists since eternity." He disagrees with the Indian estimates of the duration of time and time periods such as *kalpa*, and he disagrees also on the type of measurements used though based on the sciences of astronomy and numerology. He notes that the "Khwarizmians knew more about many constellations than the Islamic people and he gives a number of valid examples saying that it is impossible to solve astronomical questions without mathematics; he also knew well the works and achievements of the Indians. He must have been

aware of the epics since he quotes from many sources, including the *Gītā* (Al-Biruni, ed., 1997). He discusses the results of astronomical calculations, studies and quotes many Indians and their works, such as those of Āryabhaṭṭa 1st (fifth–sixth century CE), Varāhamihira and Āryabhaṭṭa 2nd (middle tenth century CE). He was critical of the "Arabs" whom he considered to be illiterate: "they do not know how to write or count and they know only numbers and what they see with the naked eye . . . while the opinions of the Indians are based on scientific observations." Nevertheless Al-Biruni is highly critical of the figures given by the Indians on the length of the *kalpas*. It would be out of place to add here much that could be said about Al-Biruni's scientific studies and work though the writings of Al-Biruni are particularly interesting from the point of view of the present essay because he refers to the Purāṇic myths as different and unique way of describing critically and accurately the results of scientific studies for the use of the non-scientist. One of the most representative in this context is the story of child Dhruv who was immortalised as the Pole Star for his firm faith in the universal presence of God as order, law and regularity in the universe.

I would close by saying that metrology and numerology are scientific facets or aspects of God Mitra.

fig 1. Imprint of a seal of the Hittite king Suppiluliuma 1st of Hatti (capital city Hattusha), middle fourteenth century BCE. See Guidotti and Daddi, 2002.

fig 2. Line drawing of the imprint of a seal of Suppiluliuma of Hatti. Reading from up downwards, highest is the solar disc which is above all Creation; under the solar disc there is a saddle-shaped seat with a flowing wing on either side. Under the seat the drawing of a belt buckle or necklace clasp (?). I would interpret the two wings as representing Mitra (Law and Justice) and Mazda (Light, Warmth). The symbol as a whole represents Ahura-Mazda or *Hvarshed (=kwarshed, Xvar-Xsahita* (Might, Splendour), the word *ahura* in Skt. corresponds to the Greek *daimon* a *Being* gifted with exceptional power and competence that he may use for good or bad.

fig. 3. Gold square "necklace button" with Ahura-Mazda shown on the "saddle" here covered by the side panel of the king's robe, from "The Hermitage", St. Petersburg; *see* Dandamayev, 1996, pre-Zarathustra period. Lining by Anna Maria Bedini.

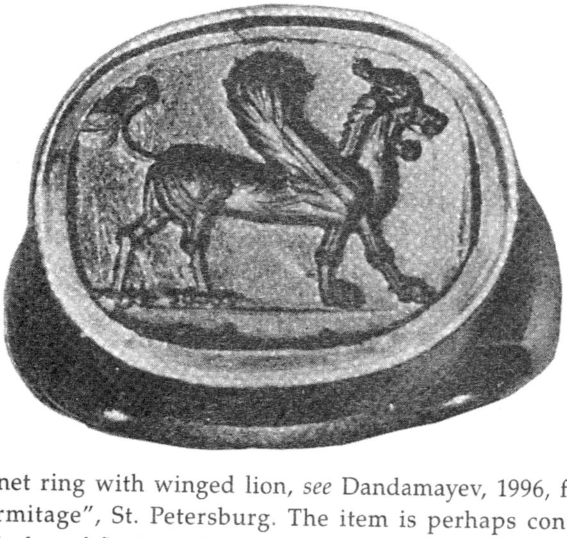

fig. 4. Signet ring with winged lion, *see* Dandamayev, 1996, from "The Hermitage", St. Petersburg. The item is perhaps contemporary with that of *fig.* 3, probably pre-Zarathustra period. Lining by Anna Maria Bedini.

fig. 5. Achaemenid king Darius 1st (558?-486? BCE) of Persia receiving a line of prisoners with a foot on a prostrated captive and the right hand held in a gesture of command. Ahura-Mazda surveys the scene from above (*see* Dandamayev, 1996).

fig. 6. Rock relief of the Investiture of Ardashir 1st at Naqsh-i-Rustam (year CE 224 or 227 — *see* Litvinsky et al., 1996; Chegini et al., 1996). The relief shows the *magus* at the extreme left waving the *barsom* and wafting the good spirit or aroma over Ardashir who holds the symbolic ring with the right hand on the opposite side and together with Ahura-Mazda.

fig. 7. Imprint from a cylinder seal showing a hunting scene with the name of Darius 1st. Ahura-Mazda with widespread wings hovers over the scene. According to authors the cuneiform script at left is probably in Aramaic language. Specially interesting details: the harnessing of the two horses, the special structure of the chariot, the shoes on the wheel and the date-palm trees.

fig. 8. *Dexiosis.* The handclasp between Mitra and the Sun-god. *From* Ossanna, 1998, front cover.

fig. 9. Tauroctony, the killing of the bull: Tauroctony, sculpture found on the altar of a Mithraeum excavated under the Basilica of St. Clement in Rome: courtesy of J. Haslett.

fig. 10. Photo of the *barsom*, contemporary specimen made of 35 metal filaments, one of them thicker, tied together with a vegetable fine string. The bundle rests horizontally over two tall metal supports placed one at each end of the bundle of "twigs". Courtesy of the Section of Anthropology and Ethnology of the Museum of Natural History of the University of Florence, Italy.

Glossary

Aditi (n) — Unlimited, boundless, mother of Infinity, the Infinite, the Universe, originator of the first seven original Ādityas.

Āditya (m) — Sons of Aditi.

Ahriman — Bad spirit or demon in the *Avesta.*

Ahura — Lord, God, giver of Life, the twelfth name that Mazda gives to himself.

Ahura-Mazda — Supreme Lord of the Universe, Zarathustra is his prophet.

Airyaman — *Yazata* of friendship, health, matrimony and wealth.

Airyanam Vaejaḥ — Ancestral homeland of all the I-A and I-I.

Aṁśa (m) — A part, a portion, one of the original seven Ādityas.

Amu-Daryā — River born in the Hindukush (Pamir), flows into the Aral Sea, river Oxus of the Greek historians.

Angra Mainyu — The Spirit of Evil, of Destruction, noxious demon. In the Khorda *Avesta* a devil that is all Death. In Phl. *Ahreman, Arimane.*

Archetype (n) —Models, ancient or ancestral types, prototypes.

Arthaśāstra (m) — Texts of knowledge, science, precepts, teachings of sacred lore.

Arya (m) — Noble, respectable person, highest caste.

Aryamān (m) — One of the late sons of Aditi, noble man, lord of the Manes or Pitṛs (ancestors).

Avesta (n) — Sacred texts of the ancient I-I, pre- and post-Zarathustra, sacred texts of Zoroastrianism and Mazdeism.

Baresman, Barsom — Originally a symbolic bunch of twigs tied together with a fine cord made of the leaflets of the plant called *barsam* (*barsom*, date-palm tree) held upright in the hand by the officiating priest at some stage of the rituals of the Zoroastrian Faith. At present in the temples the *barsom* is made of metal.

BCE — Before Christian Era.

Brahman — *Brahmā* (n) — Absolute reality, transcendent and unconditioned, Always identical to itself, One without a second.

Brahman (m) — The chief of the four priests who perform a ritualistic sacrifice whose role is to ensure that no mistakes happen throughout the entire performance of any and all sacred rituals.

Brāhmaṇa (n, sing.) — The highest of the four *varṇa*s (social order, caste).

CE — Christian Era.

Chāṇakya — (see Kauṭilya), a famous brāhmaṇa, minister of Candragupta 1st who had a leading role in the elevation of the Candragupta dynasty to their throne; ruled *c.* CE 291-315.

Chorasmia, Geogr.= Khwarizm, the Transoxiana of the Greek, part of the area between rivers Amu Daryā and Syr Daryā.

Corpus (sing., pl. corpora= literally: body) — A large collection of writings of a specific kind and subject.

Daimon — Powerful spirit having great force, may be evil or good.

Daitya — See *dānava*.

Daiva (*daeva*) (m. pl.) — In the *Avesta*: demons. Gods of the I-A. The I-I used the word deprecatingly meaning the false gods of the I-A.

Daiva (adj.) — Related to the gods, divine.

Dānava (see *daitya*) — Like the *daitya* they may be called *asura*, meaning beings gifted with exceptional power. *Dānava* are usually good and helpful.

Dexiosis or *Dexterarum conjunctio* — The two friends and partners hold their right hands firmly as a reminder of the handclasp of Mitra and Sūrya, the Sun-God later partly personified as Varuṇa (Ahura-Mazda).

Dhruv (*Dhruva*) (m) — Immobile, fixed, motionless, unwavering, permanent, the opposite of *movable* or *fickle*.

Doab — The geographic area between sister rivers such as Ganges/Indus; Tigris/Euphrates; Syr Daryā/Amu Daryā.

Draviḍian — Group of people who speak one of several very ancient Draviḍian languages such as Tamil, Malayalam, Kannada, Telugu, Oriya, Lankan, etc.

Eschatology — Branch of Theology concerned with death and/or other final events.

Euhemerism — From *Euhumerus*. Greek philosopher of the fourth century BCE who believed that gods would be or often had been men who had been or were deified by other living men because of their exceptional qualities and virtues or both.

Fibonacci, Leonardo da Pisa (1170-1240) — Of the family Fibonacci of Pisa. Author, mathematician. His best known book is the *Liber abaci* publ. 1202. The book opens with the sentence "The nine Indian ciphers are: 9, 8, 7, 6, 5, 4, 3, 2, 1. With these nine ciphers and with the sign **0** we may write any number, as demonstrated below. The mathematical symbol of the Fibonacci Number is the Greek letter *phi* that is the irrational number 1, 1, 2, 3, 5, 8, 13. . . .

Gāthā — Religious songs of the ancient I-E who migrated towards Central Asia approximately from the sixth millennium BCE or earlier and later. The most ancient migrant groups were the I-A first and the I-I somewhat later.

Gruppo Kevala — in: *Glossario Sanscrito* 1998, 2nd edn. Sanskrit Glossary ed. Asram Vidya. Roma 00165, Via Azone, 20.

Heraclides — Members of the clan or lineage of Herakles, ancient Greek hero known for his exceptional strength, the Heraclides were known for their staunch fidelity towards their clan.

Herakles — Also called Hercules in English. Extremely strong hero of the ancient Greek mythology. Son of Zeus, the immortal father and greatest among all the gods and of a mortal woman called Alcmene. Hercules was famous for his superhuman achievements, 12 of them imposed on him by the jealous Hera, consort of Zeus, are known as the 12 labours of Hercules.

Kalpa (m, n) — The length of time that lasts 14 *manvantaras* comprised between two *pralayas*; also a sacred precept, a law or ritual.

Kalpanā (f) — Mental representation, imagination.

Kavi (m) — Originally a word for poet, enlightened, wise, seer, knower of past, present and future, an epithet of the abstract concept of the Godhead; later also prince, king.

Kauṭilya — Another name of Cāṇakya, minister of Candragupta.

Khwarizm (Chorasmia) — Northern part of the doab between rivers Syr Daryā and Amu Daryā, south of the Aral Sea extended westwards as far as the Caspian Sea, north of the Karakum. Khwarizm (Chorasmia) was almost destroyed in the tenth century CE by flooding of the Amu Daryā. The new rebuilt capital Kath became the centre of a language group related to the Eastern Iranians who used the Aramaic language as regular script. Mithra was worshipped uninterruptedly from the very early periods until and after the life of Zoroaster.

Kṣatriya (m) — Member of the kṣatriya caste including royal lineages, rulers, sustainers of the Law and Justice.

Indo-Aryan (n) — Indo-Aryan, probably the first branch of the I-E people who migrated around the sixth millennium BCE into Central Asia in more than one group and at various times.

Indo-Iranian (n) — I-I, branch of the I-E people who migrated into Central Asia, closely related to the I-A. All the I-A and I-I people called themselves Arya. The differentiation between I-A and I-I arose late in the last century BCE. The name Persia and Persians became a synonym of Iran and Persia.

Indo-European (I-E) — A family of languages spoken by people presumably sharing the same origin, namely the Eurasian steppes north of the Black and Caspian Seas, from where, over the centuries they migrated into Central Asia. The term I-E comprises most of the languages of Europe as well as those of Iran, much of the Indian subcontinent and other parts of Asia. Here: ancient I-E people.

Leontocephalus (see *Narasiṁha*) — Lion-headed human figure shown as sculptures, paintings, symbols, other in most Mithraea. The creature holds a sceptre and keys in its hands. Usually shown embroiled in the coils of a serpent while in some representations a feline is shown biting at its throat. In Indian mythology it is called Narasiṁha (=man-lion), the fourth incarnation of Viṣṇu. S. Radhakrishnan (1953, 4th edn. 1974) in the Introduction to the *Īśa Upaniṣad* mentions that the purpose of the Narasiṁha *avatāra* is to teach "the essential unity of God and the world, being and becoming." The "Gruppo Kevala" (1998) agrees that the Narasiṁha *avatāra* is the symbol of consciousness as it develops fully only in human beings. Ossanna (1988) refers to many of the interpretations that Western authors have offered of the "monstrous image" that appears first in the history of the development of Western cultures at a time when the history and mythology of various cultures became closely interwoven. Ossanna further adds that the *leontocephalus* could also represent Mitra himself as seen during that stage of the development of ancient human cultures.

Magus, Magi (m) — The priestly class of the I-I in general and of the Medes, Bactrians, others.

Maitrāyaṇīya Upaniṣad — Also called *Maitri Upaniṣad* and *Kṛṣṇa Upaniṣad,* relatively modern and later than the classical Upaniṣad (S. Radhakrishnan).

Marya — Band of boisterous young men, faithful companions and armed supporters of Indra.

Mātrā — (m, n) — Measure, a measurable quantity, whatever is to be contained within limits and restrictions.

Māyā — Metaphysical ignorance, illusion.

Mazdeism — Popularly known also as Zoroastrianism, the ancient religion of the I-I and Persians, Zoroaster preached the new religion in the sixth century BCE in ancient Chorasmia/Sogdiana, present Uzbekistan.

Mazdayasna — The religion and cult of Mazda.

Mitra (m) — Latin spelling of the Sanskrit name of Āditya Mitr, the second son of Aditi.

Mithra (m) — In the *Avesta* the name refers to the *yazata* who presides over pacts and contracts; one of the great judges who sit on the *Cinvat* bridge to judge the souls of the deceased.

Mithraeum, Mithraea (n) — Lt., the temples, meeting places and sacred areas of the cult of Mitra in different languages and at different times.

Mutatis mutandis — Latin aphorism meaning: *"changing what has to be changed,"* often refers to the appropriate use of words.

Naṭarāja (m) — The Lord of Dance, Śiva dancing the *tāṇḍava* dance standing on Kāla (m, Time), symbol of unending creation, conservation and transformation of the universe and of the perfect equilibrium between life and death.

Nirukta (pp, n) — Etymology, glossary, method for the interpretation of single words leading to the understanding of the meaning not otherwise stated.

Oṁkāra (m) — The syllable *oṁ* is the symbol of all sounds including silence (*mauna*) as ātmic conscience that permeates everything.

Ormazd, Ohrmazd — Supreme god of Zoroastrianism, Ahura-Mazda of the *Avesta*: formed by Ahura=spirit + mazda, wise, meaning: wise spirit.

Pahlavī, The ancient language of Iran during the Sassanian Period, common Persian language from about 300 BCE to about CE 950; Parthia was the Latin name of the Pahlavī region.

Purāṇa (n) — "Collection of myths," collection of ancient traditions and lore, sacred texts that explain and offer commentaries, interpretations and explanations of ancient philosophical texts and myths. A very rich collection of various sorts of texts that, taken together, are the *Smṛti*, the ancient tradition memorised and repeated by human beings generation after generation, from elders to youngsters.

Ṛgveda "The Hymns" — Knowledge of the hymns, the ancient-most of the original three Vedas of the Oral Tradition.

Ṛita, — Truth, Absolute Truth, Order, Cosmic harmony. The Natural Law of the Universe.

Saṁjñāna, saṁjñā — Knowing together, share understanding, also used to designate the "general assembly".

Saguṇa Brāhman (a) — *Brahman* with attributes (*guṇa*), qualified *Brahman* or other qualified Being.

Saṁskṛta (pp) — The classical language of the ancient I-A of India, most vernacular languages and scripts of contemporary India are derived from classic Sanskrit, the script is called Devanāgarī Lipi (= a script appropriate for the gods), the classical language and script of the learned brāhmaṇas and other learned persons. It is different from vernaculars called Prākṛt that are used currently to this day.

Savitur, Savitṛ (m) — The Sun God, Supreme Light and Enlightener, the idealised Principle of Knowledge and Understanding.

Shāhnāmeh — The Epic of the kings of Persia, the famous book by Firdausi (Abdul Qasim Mansur, 940–1020).

Sogdiana — Ancient name of the southern geographic area between the Syr Daryā and the Amu Daryā rivers, later called Khwarizm.

Syr Daryā — The twin river of the Amu Daryā, born in the Tien Shan mountains, flows through the fertile Ferghana Valley and into the Aral Sea.

Tauroctony — Lt. = "the killing of the bull"; the ritual killing of the bull, actual or just symbolic. Has no ideological link with the killing of the buffalo, an ancestral rite still practised in some distant mountain areas. Mythology of later Hinduism tells of a wicked demon called Mahiṣa (Mahiṣāsura) killed by Durgā (Caṇḍī) or by Skanda in the *Mahābhārata.*

Timai, timé, (classic Gr) — Attributes, duties, jurisdiction, competence of each god as described in the Theogony of Hesiod (seventh-eighth century BCE) and other classical Greek mythological works.

Tishtrya, Syrius, star of the constellation of *Canis Major,* the brightest star in the sky. Its ascent marks the yearly flooding of the Nile and periodical events in the Indian subcontinent.

Varuṇa (m) — The One who engulfs everything in the whole universe. First and only unfettered "son" of Aditi.

Veda — Supreme knowledge, Sacred knowledge and tradition. The first of the four major Vedas: *Ṛgveda, Sāmaveda, Yajurveda, Atharvaveda.*

Verethraghna — Victory, deity who presides over victory.

Vṛtrahan, Indra Vṛtrahan — Indra, destroyer of the evil demon Vṛtra.

Yāska — Author of the *Nirukta*, oldest known glossary of the text of the Vedic hymns, lived before the time of Pāṇini fourth century BCE, Indian Sanskrit grammarian.

Yasht — Pahlavī word for hymn, book of hymns included in the Khorda *Avesta.*

Yazata — In the *Avesta*, venerable, honourable, spiritual entities, the faithful address prayers to the Yazata.

Zarathusthra, Zoroaster — Lived in the sixth century BCE and was actively preaching since year 570 BCE, reformer of Mazdeism, belonged to the Spitama family.

Bibliography

Alberti, A., 2008, *Avesta*. UTET Libreria, Torino.

Al-Biruni, It. tr. from Arabic by Giorgio De Martino 1997, *Gli Astri, il tempo, il mondo. Viaggio nell'India segreta*. edn. Xenia, Milano.

Archi, A., 2002, "Ittiti e Egiziani due colture a confronto", pp. 21-25, in: *La Battaglia di Qadesh*, M.C. Guidotti *e* F.P. Daddi, publ. Museo Archeologico Nazionale, Firenze, *figs*. 2, 3.

Bezza, G. and J. Fallis, 1997, "Introduction and bio-bibliographic profile of al-Biruni" in: *Gli Astri, il tempo, il mondo*, Ed Xenia, Milano.

Bhargava, P.L., 2001, *India in the Vedic Age*, 3rd edn., New Delhi: D.K. Printworld.

Chakravarty, U., 1997, *Indra and Other Vedic Deities*, New Delhi: D.K. Printworld.

Chegini, N.N. and A.V. Nikitin, 1996, "Sassanian Iran — Economy, Society, Arts and Crafts" in: *UNESCO: History and Civilizations of Central Asia*, vol. III, pp. 35-78.

Ciocci, A., 2003, *Luca Pacioli e la matematizzazione del sapere nel Rinascimento*, edn. Cacucci, Bari.

Cumont, F., 1900, Les mystères de Mithra, Bruxelles ; 1967, *Le religioni orientali nel paganesimo romano* (these and other quotes, *see* Ossanna 1988, Tip. Laurenziana — Napoli.

Daddi, F.P., 2002, "Muwatalli II and Fonti Ittite" in: *La Battaglia di Qadesh; Ramesse II contro gli Ittiti per la Conquista della Siria*, edn. Sillabe, Livorno.

Dandamayev, M.A., 1996, "Media and Achaemenid Iran", in: *History and Civilizations of Central Asia*, vol. II: *The Development of Sedentary and Nomadic Civilizations: 700 BC to AD 250*, UNESCO publ.

Dandekar, R.N., 1997, Pune: *Indological Miscellanea.*

———, 1979, "New Light on the Vedic God Savitṛ," in : R.N. Dandekar, *Select Writings* I, BORI.

———, 1981, "Exercises in Indology," *Select Writings* III, Ajanta Publ. Delhi at Bhandarkar Inst. Press, Pune.

Dani, A.H. and B.A. Litvinsky, 1996, "The Kushano-Sassanian Kingdom," in *History and Civilization of Central Asia: The Crossroads of Civilizations, AD 250 to 750*, vol. III, UNESCO, pp. 103-109.

Devoto, G. 1968, *Dizionario Etimologico*, Felice Le Monnier, Firenze.

Dowson, J. 1973, *A Classical Dictionary of Hindu Mythology and Religion, Geography: History and Literature*, Oriental Books Reprint Corporation, Munshiram Manoharlal, New Delhi.

Edel, E. 1998, Korrespondenz, Paris 1987, *Die aegyptisch-hethitische Korrespondenz aus Boghazkoi in babilonischer und hethitischer Sprache*, vols. I-II, Opladen 1994.

Firdausi, Abul Kasim (or) Qasim Mansur of Khorasan, 940-1030, author of *Shah Namah* (The Epic of the Kings).

Ghirshman, R. 1977, *l'Iran et la migration des Indo-Aryens et des Iraniens*, Leiden: E.J. Brill.

Glossario Sanscrito, a cura del gruppo Kevala, 1988, 2nd edn., Roma, Via Azone 20, Ashram Vidya.

Griffith, R.T.H, 1889 (last edn. 1986), *The Hymns of the Ṛgveda*, Motilal Banarsidass.

Guidotti, M.C. and F.P. Daddi (edn.), 2002, *La Battaglia di Qadesh, Ramesse II contro gli Ittiti per la conquista della Siria*, Museo Archeologico Nazionale, Firenze, edn. Sillabe [*Iconography of the Battle of Qadesh*, courtesy of National Museum of Archaeology, Firenze), p. 23.

Jung, C.G. first publ. 1961, last edn. 2006, *Ricordi, Sogni, Riflessioni*, edn. BUR (Biblioteca Universale Rizzoli), Italy.

———, 1996, *La Psicologia del Kundalini Yoga*, Italian edn. by Sonu Shamdasani, Bollati Boringhieri, Torino.

———, 2008, 1st edn. 1997, last edn. 2008 in: *Opere di Carl G. Jung*, vol. 9, part 1 and part 2, ed. Bollati Boringhieri Torino.

Laureano, P. 1993, *Giardini di pietra, I Sassi di Matera e la Civiltā Mediterranea*. Bollati Boringhieri, Torino.

———, 1998, *La piramide rovesciata. Il modello dell'oasi per il pianeta Terra*. Bollati Boringhieri, Torino.

———, 1999, *Agua: el ciclo de la vida, Lala Libros, Barcelona.*

———, 2001, *Atlante d'Acqua. Conoscenze tradizionali per la lotta alla desertificazione*, Bollati Boringhieri, Torino.

———, 2001, *Sahara, Oasi e deserto*, Giunti Industrie Grafiche S.P.A. Prato.

Lévi, Strauss, 2009, *La dottrina del sacrificio nei Braahmana*, Adelphi, S.P.A., Milano.

Levy, Reuben, 1967, *The Epic of the Kings: Shah Namah*, The National Epic of Persia by Firdausi, Univ. Press Chicago.

Litvinsky, B.A., 1996, Cities and Urban Life in the Kushan Kingdom, chap. 13, UNESCO, *History of Civilizations of Central Asia*; v. II, 700 BCE-CE 250, pp. 291-12.

Liverani, M., 1988, Antico Oriente. Storia. Società, Economia, edn. Laterza and Figli S.P.A.

———, 1998, Le *lettere di el-Amarna*, vols. 1-2, Brescia 1998 edn. Padeia.

———, 2009, *Antico oriente. Storia, società, economia*. edn. Laterza, SEDIT, Bari, per conto Gius.Laterza and Figli, S.p.a. Roma, Bari.

Livio, M., 2002, *The Golden Ratio*. It. edn. 2003, *La sezione aurea*, RCS Libri S.p.a., Milano.

Mazumdar, R.C., 1988, *The Vedic Age*, Bharatiya Vidya Bhavan, New Delhi.

Mazumdar, S., 2005, *Tales from the Purāṇas*, Bharatiya Vidya Bhavan, New Delhi.

Monte, G.F. del, 1993, *L'annalistica Ittita*, ed. Paideia, Brescia, p. 153.

Moran, W.L. 1987, *Les lettres de el-Amarna*, Paris.

Nerazik, E.E. and P.G. Bulgakov, 1996, "Khwarizm (P.G. Bulgakov)," in: *History of Civilizations of Central Asia*, vol. III: *The Crossroad of Civilizations*, AD *250 to 750*, UNESCO.

Ossanna, T., 1988, *La stretta di mano, il contenuto etico della religione di Mitra*. edn. Borla, Tipografia Laurenziana, Napoli.

Purchas, S., 1864, *Early Travels in India: 16th and 17th Centuries*, re-edited 1974. Deep Publ. Delhi.

Radhakrishnan, S., 1974 (1st edn. 1953), *The Principal Upaniṣads*, Muirhead Library of Philosophy, ed. H.D. Lewis, London, George Allen and Unwin Ltd.

Raphael, 2nd edn. 2004, *Orfismo e Tradizione iniziatica*, ed. Ashram Vidya, Via Azone 20, Roma.

Rogers, A., 2002 (1st edn. 1907), *The Shah-Namah of Fardusi*, Low Price Publ., Delhi.

Schiltz, V., 1991, *Histoire des Kourgans, La redécouverte de l'or des Scythes*, Gallimard, Paris.

Tertulliano, D.S.F. Opere Scelte, 1974, *a cura Moreschini*, C. Torino, 1974.

Vannucci, M., 1998, *The Origin of the Cult of Demeter: The Story of Hexaploid Wheat*, Bhandarkar Oriental Research Institute, pp. 83-114.

———, 1999, *Human Ecology in the Vedas*, New Delhi: D.K. Printworld.

———, 2004, *Life in India*, New Delhi: Virgo Publ.

———, 2007, *Ancient Gods and Heroes of East and West*, New Delhi: D.K. Printworld.

———, forthcoming, *The Evolution of the Cultures of Central Asia.*

Wheeler, J.T. 1974 (see S. Purchas).

Index